# The Book of
# FLOWER
# GARDENING

Above: Even a small area in poor soil can be rich in variety and
interest. This border includes pinks, stachys and the woolly 'lamb's
ear' foliage of verbascum, all of which — given sun and good
drainage — will flourish in almost any soil.
Overleaf: Elegant tulips, with their ramrod-straight stems and vivid
flowers, offer the perfect foil to feathery masses of springtime
foliage.
Endpapers: A spectacular colour composition in a summertime
border. The eye-catching golden-orange of the eschscholzia
(Californian poppy) complements the surrounding blues, pinks
and purples.

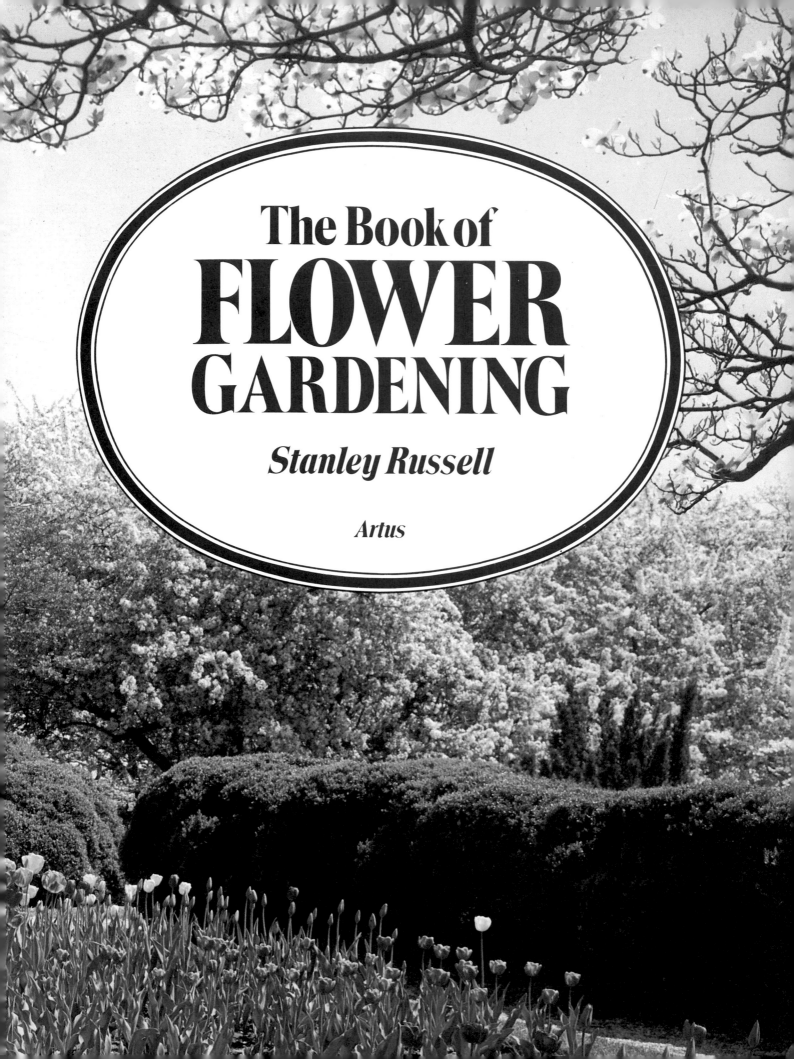

# The Book of
# FLOWER
# GARDENING

## Stanley Russell

### Artus

# Contents

## Introduction
**The whole plant**
page 7

## 1 *Annuals and Biennials*
**Summer colour from seeds**
page 11

## 2 *Bulbs*
**Versatile storage plants**
page 45

© Stanley Russell, 1978

Reprinted January 1979

First published in 1978 by Artus Publishing Company Ltd
91 Clapham High Street, London SW4 7TF

Printed in Great Britain by Jarrold and Sons Ltd, Norwich

## 3 *Perennials*
**Years of colour from seed or cuttings**
page 69

## 4 *Shrubs and Trees*
**Your garden in outline**
page 93

## 5 *Roses Old and New*
**The universal favourites**
page 129

# Introduction

## The whole plant

**F**lowers and decorative foliage plants have an important role in all our lives. They do not serve the practical function of providing us with food, but they do form a living part of many homes and offices and are an essential part of our personal environment.

The garden can offer us a great variety of plants and flowers to enjoy. There are the herbaceous plants: the annuals and biennials, usually started from seed, and the perennials, which come from seed, cuttings, or division of established clumps. There are bulbs, which are planted in autumn and spring, providing welcome early colour and (particularly with lilies and gladioli) statuesque grandeur. And there are shrubs and trees, that vast army of labour-savers that take a little time to establish themselves and reach maturity but then, as a rule, require little or no maintenance.

Plants reward the gardener with a fine display of colour, and often perfume. Their power to please is immense; their range and scope is bounded only by the space available and the confines of the gardener's own imagination. Yet the cold fact is that really the flower is not there for our benefit at all. It is part of the plant's own struggle for survival. Its colour, and any perfume, are mainly to attract pollinating insects so that it can produce seeds and continue its own race.

In general, plants are propagated either by seed or vegetatively – that is by cuttings or roots taken from the parent. Like all tender young life, they have to be cosseted in their early stages. They require, apart from warmth to make them comfortable, a correctly proportioned diet of nutrient from the soil or compost. In time, they reach maturity, giving pleasure to the eye and to the nose and the palate, but as the year progresses decay sets in. The petals and the foliage die and fall to earth, many of them to be dragged down by the worms. The worms aerate and benefit the soil in the process, and the leaves provide working capital for the bacteria to enrich the soil so the next season's plants can thrive.

This may be an over-simplification of the cycle, but it is broadly both accurate and universal, for it applies to all plants in their seasons. The flowering plants have a further responsibility from an early stage in their career, for they secrete in their blooms a very fine dust that is collected by pollinating insects and transferred to other plants. This provides the essential extra ingredient that makes them bear fruit, whether it be edible for humans or the seed from which the next generation will come. Some plants are self-pollinating; others

Left and below: Two very different garden borders: a flower border in high summer, with 'Iceberg' roses, yellow pansies, golden achillea and dianthus; and (below) foliage plants, including silver-leaved cineraria, maritima and multi-coloured coleus.

Right: The popular hybrid tea rose 'Peace', introduced in America at the end of the Second World War.

## The whole plant

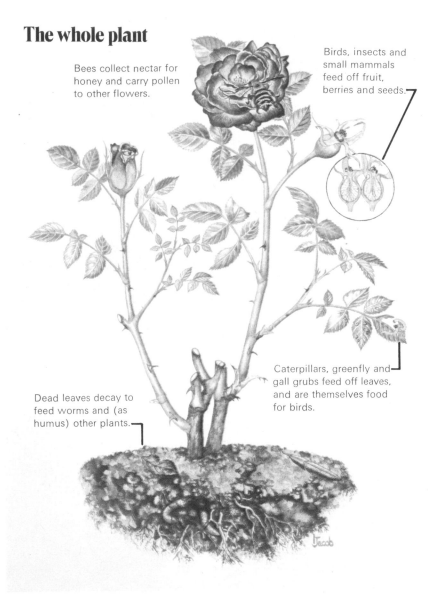

Bees collect nectar for honey and carry pollen to other flowers.

Birds, insects and small mammals feed off fruit, berries and seeds.

Caterpillars, greenfly and gall grubs feed off leaves, and are themselves food for birds.

Dead leaves decay to feed worms and (as humus) other plants.

have to be crossed with pollen from a different breed, and this – again over-simplifying – is the origin of all plant life.

All garden plants contribute to the ecology. The annuals, which grow, mature, and die all in one season; the biennials, sown in one year, to mature in the next; and the perennials, which go on apparently for ever – each of these plants settles its debt yearly by ensuring a supply of food for its neighbours and successors.

Most of today's cultivated varieties have their origins in the wild flowers that inhabited the globe before humanity became civilized. One of the more praiseworthy of man's achievements over the centuries has been to help the propagation and improvement process. In doing so he has produced millions of plants that give so much pleasure it would be a pity to let them merely fade and die. A huge world-wide industry has been created, which in effect results in the vast majority of the flowers that grow being surplus to Nature's requirements for the reproduction process. So we have this enormous range of blooms available to delight us, either on site where they are growing or indoors to provide a vast and ever-changeable decorative display.

The great appeal of the ornamental plant is that in all but a comparatively few cases, little skill is required on the part of the grower. Generally, he has to provide just the right soil and reasonable conditions. There is a great temptation when starting a garden to pack it with what *you* want to grow. You won't get a good result unless the plants co-operate, and they will make their own terms.

The first, and obvious one, is that the soil must suit them. The classic examples here are the rhododendron and azalea, which will thrive on a diet of acid from a peaty soil but will make no progress if imprisoned in chalk. So study your soil, take samples from every few square metres (the structure and type can vary astonishingly) and carry out a few simple tests with the equipment that can be bought at most garden shops. A good plan is to see what is being grown successfully in your locality. Don't be put off if you cannot see what you want; it may be merely that nobody else has thought of your idea.

The rules for obtaining a successful display are few and fairly straightforward. In spite of what has been said, the great majority of plants will survive, if not prosper, in most kinds of soil; only a comparative few have idiosyncrasies about peat, chalk or sand. But there are certain

# Starting from seed: a guide to the basic principles

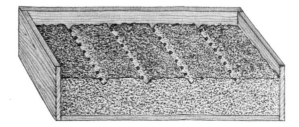

**1** Sow seed sparsely in drills in seeding compost.

**2** Cover with a fine layer of seeding compost and press down.

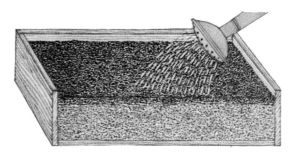

**3** Water lightly and leave to germinate.

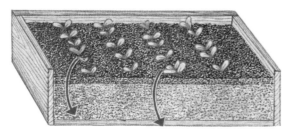

**4** After germination, remove weak and overcrowded seedlings.

**5** When the second pair of leaves appears, prick the seedlings out to a prepared pot or bed. Ease the roots gently from the compost, holding the seedling by the leaves.

requirements, or at least preferences, concerning position and situation. Some – most of the rock plants – like a dry situation; others, like the mosses, prefer damp conditions. Other extremes are the sunflower, needing all the sun it can get, and the lily of the valley, capable of making a shady corner a bright one.

The whole operation of gardening is very simple. The gift of so-called green fingers is as much one of commonsense as anything: the wider knowledge of names and varieties and their individual quirks comes with experience. But all of us, novice and expert alike, experience the same thrill when we see a shoot emerge, or a bud form, or a leaf unfurl. We don't have to understand plants and flowers to get tremendous enjoyment from them, for their variety

and range is infinite – and the ability to enjoy such an infinite range is one of the many rewards all gardeners have.

Practical advice on planning and planting is given in each chapter, and general information is followed by information on specific species and varieties. Naturally I have had to be selective and my choice is largely a personal one of plants I have grown, or am particularly fond of, or regard as deserving to be better known. Tables at the end of each chapter provide an easy reference guide to the requirements and characteristics of each of the plants mentioned.

Finally, for those who wish to explore further, and perhaps find unusual or rare plants for the garden, I have included a short bibliography.

# 1 *Annuals and Biennials*

## Summer colour from seeds

The simplest method of doing something is usually the best, and a garden provides plenty of evidence proving the truth of this assertion. What could be simpler than strewing a few seeds on a patch of bare soil in springtime and being rewarded a few weeks later with a mass of colourful bloom that will last until the frosts of autumn? It is a quick and satisfactory way of starting a garden from scratch and seeing it mature in its first summer.

The gardener growing for amenity purposes – flowers and foliage for pleasure as distinct from vegetables and edible fruits – has two main fields of operation: shrubs, distinguished by their woody growth, and herbaceous subjects, which have softer and mainly green stems. The herbaceous plants are in turn broken down into three sub-sections.

Annuals are grown from seed; they flower, set seed, and die within a few months. Generally, as the name implies, this is within a year, but in practice some can be started in mid- or late summer one year to flourish longer and more strongly the next.

Biennials, also grown from seed, differ from annuals in that they take two years to complete their life cycle. The roots remain alive at the end of their first season, to give bloom the following year, and then they die.

The third group, perennials, have mostly started from seed like the others and die down at the end of the season. But their roots survive more or less permanently and the flowers grow again every year. They form a very large part of the herbaceous scene and are dealt with separately in a later chapter. Many perennials are also grown as biennials, and some even as annuals, for a quick start. All very confusing, but what it means is that there are no really hard and fast divisions, so the gardener gets the benefit of whatever the plant can offer.

There is a further large and important section of plants qualifying as herbaceous in the sense that they are non-woody: bulbs. It is possible to start bulbous plants from seed, but this is a very long process and for practical purposes is ignored by the amateur, except that he can plant dahlia corms that he had started as seed barely twelve months earlier. Bulbs, nevertheless, do claim a large following because of their year-round application, and they, too, have a chapter to themselves.

Here we are concentrating on the quick-growing army of plants that transform bare patches of soil in early spring into a kaleidoscope of colour by summer: the annuals and the biennials, or plants grown as such. They can be sown as seed in the greenhouse, or even indoors,

Left: Pink geranium 'King of Denmark', planted here with nemesia and 'Excelsior' hybrid foxgloves.

Below: *Dianthus × allwoodii* 'Doris'. The allwoodii pinks have an astonishing range of colour and form and need only dead-heading to bloom throughout the summer.

Few plants give more pleasure, indoors or out, than the sweet pea, *Lathyrus odoratus*. The scented varieties have a delicious perfume, and the extra trouble in growing them on the cordon system is well repaid by the longer stems, making them ideal for table decoration. Daily picking encourages greater flowering.

and hardened off in a cool but protected area before being planted out, or they can be sown a little later where they are intended to bloom. If you are late in starting, or do not want the bother of raising from seed, you can buy bedding plants, which have been germinated under heat in a nursery. The drawback with this last method is that you have to take what the nurseryman has in stock, which will very often be limited to a small number of profitable lines. There are a few dedicated specialists who offer unusual plants, but generally if you want something a little out of the ordinary you will have to buy the seed and raise it yourself.

Never buy bedding plants that are limp and long-legged: they have not been properly looked after. Either they have been given too much light, or not enough, or they have been put out into the open too soon and not hardened off properly. You often see boxes of plants outside greengrocers' shops, subjected to a bitterly cold wind; most of them will be lucky to survive, let alone prosper. Pick strong, sturdy-legged plants with stiff, healthy leaves. When handling very young seedlings always hold them by a leaf, never by the tender stem.

One point we tend to overlook about flower seed is that annuals give a better show per plant

than the biennials and perennials. This is not necessarily because they are better plants, but is a clue to the struggle for existence. As we have seen, an annual flowers and dies within a single year. It has no reserves of life; the roots have no means of storing energy when the stem dies down. For the breed to continue, therefore, there must be an adequate reservoir of seed. This is achieved by a burst of flower far greater in proportion than with any other of the herbaceous types.

So annuals are not being obligingly prolific for our interest and enjoyment. It is an attempt to make sure there is enough potential to withstand the hazards of winter: cold soil resulting in poor germination, and the depredations of seed-hungry birds and mice foraging for food.

It has been estimated that the seed accounts for half the weight of an annual plant at the end of the season, and when you reflect that each seed, light as it is, is really a complete though dormant new plant, you realize that the annuals do give themselves a fair chance of survival!

There is a further herbaceous sub-division, into hardy and half-hardy plants. The terms apply to annuals, biennials and perennials alike and mean, briefly, seeds that can be sown outside directly into the soil (hardy) and those that need some protection and gentle warmth to enable them to germinate (half-hardy).

The hardy annuals are the simplest of all plants. They are quick-growing, can be sown in the open ground when the soil warms up (in Britain this normally means between March and May), and thinned out if necessary. The half-hardies are usually started earlier in a heated greenhouse to aid germination and are then hardened off in an unheated but protected area, such as a cold frame, before being planted out. This can be done as seedlings (when only the two seed-leaves have appeared) or as bedding plants. With some you can take a chance, delay a couple of months or so and treat them as hardies, trusting to luck and a good summer that they will come into flower, even if later than the scheduled time.

Unfortunately, if you are dealing with a plant whose seed cannot be sown successfully until, say, May, you cannot expect it to flower before June and by then you are at the height of summer. Many will be in bloom for no more than three weeks, possibly less, but you can prolong the flowering season to some extent by successional sowing, at weekly or fortnightly intervals.

The sweet william is a member of the dianthus group, related to carnations and pinks, but the perfume is restricted to the biennial and perennial varieties: the annuals have lost their scent.

| NAME | HEIGHT | | SITUATION | USES | COLOUR | IN FLOWER | | | | | | | | |
| | cm | ft | | | | M | A | M | J | J | A | S | O | N |
|---|---|---|---|---|---|---|---|---|---|---|---|---|---|---|
| Ageratum | 15 | ½ | sun | edging | blue | | | | ❀ | ❀ | ❀ | ❀ | ❀ | |
| Althaea (Hollyhock) | 200 | 6½ | sun | cutting | pink, red, yellow, white | | | | ❀ | ❀ | ❀ | | | |
| Alyssum | 10 | ½ | sun, rockery | edging, box | white, pink, purple | | | | ❀ | ❀ | ❀ | | | |
| Amaranthus | 100 | 3½ | damp, shade | cutting | purple, greenish yellow; green and crimson/yellow leaves | | | | ❀ | ❀ | ❀ | | | |
| Antirrhinum | 20–90 | ½–3 | sun, rockery | cutting, border | mixed | | | | ❀ | ❀ | ❀ | ❀ | ❀ | |
| Aster | 45–90 | 1½–3 | sun, part shade | cutting | blue, pink, purple, red, yellow, white | | | ❀ | ❀ | ❀ | ❀ | ❀ | | |
| Begonia semperflorens | 15–20 | 6–8 | sheltered | edging, box | pink, red, white | | | | | | ❀ | ❀ | ❀ | |
| Bellis perennis | 20 | ½ | sun, part shade | edging | mixed | | | | ❀ | | | | | |
| Calceolaria | 20–30 | ½–1 | shade | box, tubs, edging | yellow, bronze | | | | ❀ | ❀ | | | | |
| Calendula | 30 | 1 | sun, part shade | border | yellow/orange | | | | ❀ | ❀ | ❀ | ❀ | ❀ | |
| Celosia (Cockscomb) | 30 | 1 | dry, sun | border | pink, red, crimson, yellow, white, cream | | | | | ❀ | ❀ | ❀ | | |
| Cheiranthus (Wallflower) | 45 | 1½ | sun, wall | cutting, border | red, crimson, purple, yellow | ❀ | ❀ | | ❀ | ❀ | ❀ | ❀ | | ❀ |
| Chrysanthemum | 45–90 | 1½–3 | sun | cutting | red, maroon, yellow, white | | | | ❀ | ❀ | ❀ | ❀ | ❀ | ❀ |
| Cobaea scandens (Cup-&-saucer plant) | 300–500 | 10–17 | sunny wall, trellis | climber | green, purple-blue | | | | ❀ | ❀ | ❀ | ❀ | | |
| Convolvulus | 15–200 | ½–6½ | sun | border or climber | purple, blue, crimson/white | | | | ❀ | ❀ | ❀ | | | |
| Cosmos | 120 | 4 | damp, shade | cutting | orange, red | | | | | | ❀ | ❀ | ❀ | |
| Dahlia | 60–120 | 2–4 | sun | cutting | mixed | | | | ❀ | ❀ | ❀ | ❀ | | |
| Delphinium (Larkspur) | 150 | 5 | sun | cutting | blue, red | | | | ❀ | ❀ | | | | |
| Dianthus (Carnation, Pink, Sweet william) | 15–75 | ½–2½ | mainly sun | cutting, box | mixed | | | ❀ | ❀ | ❀ | ❀ | ❀ | | |
| Dimorphotheca (Star of the veldt) | 25 | 1 | dry, sun | cutting | white, pink, yellow, bronze | | | ❀ | | | | | | |
| Euphorbia lathyrus (Caper spurge) | 120 | 4 | shade | border | green and yellow/white leaves, non-flowering | | | | | | | | | |
| Gaillardia (Blanket flower) | 50–100 | 1½–3½ | dry, sun | cutting | red, yellow | | | | | ❀ | ❀ | ❀ | | |
| Gazania | 40 | 1½ | dry, sun | edging, pots | yellow, orange | | | | ❀ | ❀ | ❀ | ❀ | | |
| Godetia | 35–70 | 1–2½ | sun | box, edging | red, pink, orange, lavender | | | | | ❀ | ❀ | ❀ | ❀ | |
| Helianthus (Sunflower) | 120–200 | 4–6½ | dry, sun | cutting | yellow | | | | | | ❀ | ❀ | | |
| Helichrysum (Straw flower) | 30–60 | 1–2 | sun | cutting | red, yellow, white | | | | | ❀ | ❀ | | | |
| Heliotrope (Cherry pie) | 60 | 2 | sun | border | purple, blue | | | | | ❀ | ❀ | ❀ | | |
| Humulus japonicus (Hop plant) | 300 | 10 | sun | climber | green and white/yellow leaves | | | | ❀ | ❀ | ❀ | | | |
| Lathyrus odoratus (Sweet pea) | 100–200 | 3½–6½ | dry, sun | climber, cutting | mixed | | | | ❀ | ❀ | ❀ | ❀ | | |
| Lavatera (Mallow) | 120 | 4 | sun | cutting | white, pink | | | | | ❀ | ❀ | ❀ | | |
| Lobelia | 15 | ½ | sun, part shade | edging, box | blue, purple, red, white | | | | ❀ | ❀ | ❀ | ❀ | | |
| Lunaria (Honesty) | 60 | 2 | shade | cutting | purple, silver pods | | | ❀ | ❀ | ❀ | | | | |
| Lupinus (Lupin) | 30–120 | 1–4 | dry, sun | cutting | mixed | | | | ❀ | ❀ | | | | |
| Matthiola (Stock) | 30 | 1 | shade | cutting | mixed | | | | ❀ | ❀ | ❀ | | | |
| Mimulus (Monkey flower) | 15 | ½ | damp, shade | rockery | yellow | | | | ❀ | ❀ | ❀ | | | |
| Molucella (Bells of Ireland) | 100 | 3½ | sun | cutting | green, cream leaves, non-flowering | | | | | | | | | |
| Myosotis (Forget-me-not) | 20 | ½ | damp, shade | edging | blue | ❀ | ❀ | ❀ | ❀ | | | | | |
| Nemesia | 30 | 1 | dry, sun | box | mixed | | | | ❀ | ❀ | ❀ | ❀ | | |
| Nicotiana (Tobacco plant) | 60 | 2 | damp, shade | border | purple, pink, crimson, white, green | | | | ❀ | ❀ | ❀ | ❀ | | |
| Nigella (Love-in-a-mist) | 50 | 1½ | damp | cutting | blue, pink, lilac, white, red | | | | ❀ | ❀ | ❀ | | | |
| Petunia | 25 | 1 | dry, sun | box | blue, pink, purple, red, white | | | | ❀ | ❀ | ❀ | ❀ | | |
| Phlox drummondii | 25–40 | 1–1½ | part shade | cutting, box | mixed | | | ❀ | ❀ | ❀ | ❀ | ❀ | | |
| Rudbeckia (Cone flower) | 50–100 | 1½–3½ | dry, sun | cutting | yellow, red, bronze | | | | ❀ | ❀ | ❀ | ❀ | | |
| Salpiglossis | 60 | 2 | sun | cutting | mixed | | | | ❀ | ❀ | ❀ | | | |
| Salvia | 25–45 | 1–1½ | dry, sun | cutting | red, pink, purple, white | | | | ❀ | ❀ | ❀ | ❀ | | |
| Senecio cineraria | 30 | 1 | dry, sun | edging | silver leaves | | | | ❀ | ❀ | ❀ | | | |
| Statice (Sea pink) | 60 | 2 | sun | cutting | mixed | | | ❀ | ❀ | ❀ | ❀ | ❀ | | |
| Tagetes (Marigold) | 20–60 | ½–2 | sun | edging | orange, yellow | | | | ❀ | ❀ | ❀ | ❀ | ❀ | |
| Tagetas erecta | 90 | 3 | sun | cutting | orange, yellow | | | | ❀ | ❀ | ❀ | ❀ | | |
| Thunbergia | 120 | 4 | sun, sheltered | climber | white, yellow, orange | | | | ❀ | ❀ | ❀ | | | |
| Tropaeolum (Nasturtium) | 15–200 | ½–6½ | damp | climber, box | red, orange, yellow | | | | ❀ | ❀ | ❀ | ❀ | ❀ | |
| Verbena | 30 | 1 | sun | cutting, edging | red, pink, purple, blue, yellow | | | | ❀ | ❀ | ❀ | ❀ | | |
| Viola (Viola & Pansy) | 20 | ½ | damp, shade | border | mixed | | | | ❀ | ❀ | ❀ | ❀ | | |
| Zinnia | 90 | 3 | dry, sun | cutting | red, orange, pink, yellow | | | | ❀ | ❀ | ❀ | ❀ | | |
| Zinnia (dwarf) | 25 | 1 | dry, sun | edging | red, orange, pink, yellow | | | | ❀ | ❀ | ❀ | ❀ | | |

The lack of flowers in spring and early summer is a matter for regret, but there are other means of filling the space effectively, as the following chapters demonstrate. The important factor is that throughout the longest and warmest days of the year your garden can be filled very cheaply and most satisfactorily with annuals and biennials.

And when they do appear, what a wide range they cover! You can use them as edging at the front of a border; you can have them filling beds and borders on their own; you can have them climbing up fences, walls and trellises or hanging gracefully from baskets and window boxes. You can have them reflecting the sun or bringing cool grace to a shady corner. You can alternate between clusters of tiny flowers no bigger than a thumb nail and massive blooms 10cm (4in) in diameter – or more, and you can plan a floral display at any height from 10cm (4in) to 120cm (4ft) or more. Some have no

flowers worth mentioning but score heavily with the magnificence of their leaf colouring. Some have a subtle perfume to add to their beauty of form. There are even a few that offer fragrance from the leaf. As for colour, you can have every shade except jet black, and doubtless it will not be many years before even that is achieved.

One of the many attributes of annuals and biennials is that they ask for little attention. Given freedom from pests something will show from seed sown even in the poorest soil. Naturally, some previous attention in preparing the area will prove beneficial, but this need not be of an elaborate nature. All that is necessary is to dig over the soil beforehand – the previous autumn clean-up time is ideal – work in a little manure or compost and, for long-term benefit, some slow-acting bone meal. Level the ground and rake it to a fine tilth just before sowing, so that there are only tiny particles of soil, in which

A massed planting of geraniums and alyssum, with pink ivy-leaved pelargoniums and blue lobelia, makes an effective display for a hanging basket.

the seed can lie comfortably without being suspended in an air pocket. Remember that seed must be in contact with the soil, so that the bacteria there can get on with their work of bringing it to life.

With half-hardies, or other plants germinated in a seed tray in the greenhouse for extra starting warmth, the procedure is similar but on a smaller scale. The seed is placed in the fine compost, covered lightly with it, and kept dark until germination so that the sun does not dry out the compost.

Some seed, bought in pelleted form, looks huge, being coated with a clay-like substance. Pelleted seeds are more expensive but carry some benefit as they are easier to handle and involve less wastage, for the thinning-out chore is either greatly reduced or eliminated altogether. They usually take a little longer to germinate because the coating has to be broken down by the moisture in the soil, so it is helpful to depart from the usual rule and give a light watering immediately after sowing. 'Light' is the important word, for the clay material absorbs moisture and if there is too much it becomes a sticky mess that could prevent the emergence of the seedling.

There is another, and smaller, category of seeds known as tender annuals, or greenhouse biennials. These need a somewhat higher temperature in their early stages of germination and are mainly for the greenhouse or conservatory. They are usually grown in pots, but some make colourful and valuable contributions to an outside border. Among them are such favourites as calceolaria, cineraria, primulas, begonias, pelargoniums, coleus and impatiens (balsam or busy lizzie), a list sufficiently imposing to underline the fact that although a greenhouse may not be, strictly speaking, part of a garden, it is an essential part of the equipment of any serious gardener. It enables him to produce a far greater range of plants (and also prolong his colour season all the year round) than would otherwise be the case'.

For the purpose of this chapter, I have divided annuals and biennials into four sections, based on their size. The first consists of plants for the rock garden or the front of a bed or border: the edging plants. I have, somewhat arbitrarily, limited these to plants that will normally be below 25cm (10in) in height. The second category is the border plants, from 25 to 60cm (10in to 2ft), which will usually be in the middle of the border. It follows that the third class is the 'giants' for the back of the border, for

Left: A rock garden in spring, with brilliant colour supplied by aubrietia, saxifrage, golden alyssum and mixed conifers.

whom 60cm (2ft) would be regarded as stunted. This section includes the climbers. The fourth category, irrespective of height, deals with plants noted particularly for their foliage or bracts as distinct from the actual flower.

## Edging or Rock Garden Plants
Up to 25cm (10in)

### Ageratum (hha)
A low-growing edging or rock garden plant that rarely grows above 15cm (6in), which makes it ideal for edging, while providing excellent colour. Given regular dead-heading, it will continue to thrive until the frosts. The clusters of small, mostly blue, flowers go remarkably well with marigolds (blue and orange or yellow make a striking colour partnership). There is a white variety, and also a reddish-mauve shade.

### Alyssum (ha)
Most people probably associate alyssum with lobelia. Very sweet-smelling, almost to the point of being sickly, its tiny blooms are equally ideal for the front of the bed or for filling the crevices in a rock garden. It will bloom all through the summer, and most varieties never reach above 10cm (4in). It is available in white, pink or purple. A new variety, 'Wonderland', has won an award for consistency of flower and is a very dark red, so dark that sometimes it is difficult to see it against the soil. (See also page 76.)

Right: *Calceolaria multiflora grandiflora*, a greenhouse perennial.

Below: *Begonia semperflorens*, the small-flowered fibrous rooted types (easily grown from seed), flower prolifically and are ideal for borders and containers. They are weather-resistant and continue in bloom for many weeks.

### Anchusa (ha)
A mass of deep blue flowers gives a low carpet of colour. Ask for 'Blue Angel', otherwise you may get a perennial version that grows to six times the size. (See also page 85.)

### Asperula (ha) Woodruff
One of the lesser-known edging or rock garden plants. It grows to about 15cm (6in) with clusters of scented mauve-blue flowers.

### Begonia semperflorens
Begonias come in two types, tuberous and fibrous rooted, which can be rather confusing to the non-expert. The tuberous kind are dealt with in the next chapter. The fibrous rooted make up in quantity what they lack in quality, but are nonetheless delightful little flowers with excellent bronze-green foliage. *B. semperflorens* is a dwarf plant, marvellous for bedding schemes. I keep some in a trough by my front door, and almost everyone who visits us in summer remarks on their attractive colours. The leaves are a pleasure in themselves, but it is the mass of mixed colour – pinks, reds, and whites – that is the big point in their favour. Given luck, some shelter, sunshine, and not too much rain, they will flower continuously until the frosts. (See also page 60.)

### Calceolaria
Some varieties are listed as annuals and others as biennials, but all should be started in a greenhouse. It has a speckled, pouch-type flower, ranging from 15 to 30cm (6 to 12in) in height, usually yellow or orange. It is extremely

useful for mixing with other plants and is good for tubs and window boxes as well. Sow in February in warmth. The seed is very fine and expensive, so don't waste it. It costs (at the time of writing) £26 a gram, but you won't need all this as you would have to find room for something like 45,000 plants!

## Dianthus

There are three favourite types of dianthus, the little pinks and sweet williams, and the taller carnations. All are traditional cottage garden plants, and well beloved still, but they do challenge the cultural expertise of the new gardener. Sweet william, for instance, can be either a hardy annual or a half-hardy perennial (usually grown as a biennial), and to avoid disappointment you must know which type you want, or have. The flowers all look much alike, mostly in shades of pink, red or purple, either self-coloured or zoned, but the annuals, at 20cm (8in), are barely half the height of the perennials. Although the biennials (or perennials grown as such) retain the scent that gave them their name, I cannot recall finding an annual variety that fulfils the claim. Nevertheless, their frilled petals are so pretty and attractive that one can forgive them anything.

The pinks (some of which are white) are normally used as annuals, either hardy or half-hardy, but there is a hardy biennial strain, and even a perennial. The carnations, on the other hand, are nominally biennials or perennials, but with some of them, seed sown under glass in February and planted out towards the end of May will produce splendid blooms in time for the holiday season. You see how confusing it is!

In general the sweet williams and pinks are recommended for borders and as edging plants; indeed, some pinks are so dwarf that they excel in rockeries. 'Persian Carpet' at 10cm (4in), is ideal for this purpose and comes in a colour range that includes pink, scarlet, cerise and white. Among the taller versions of the pinks are two F$_1$ (first generation) hybrids that have won awards in the All-America trials – 'Magic Charms', a dwarf 15–20cm (6–8in), and 'Queen of Hearts' 30–45cm (12–18in).

Carnations vary in size from about 30cm (1ft) to 75cm (2½ft) and are among the grandest of our scented flowers. Weddings would not be the same without them! The perfume, usually described as clove-like, is unmistakable and makes their corner of the garden (or the room) a place in which to linger. They are white, pink, vivid red, or even purple. Additionally, there

are the picotee kinds, with a band of different colour around the edge of the petals. The familiar clove scent is common to all types, but the perpetual flowering ones somewhat belie their name as they are slightly delicate and should be grown in the greenhouse. For outdoor work, specify the hardy type known as border carnations. (See also pages 77 and 90.)

## Dimorphotheca (ha) Star of the veldt
See *Tagetes*.

Pinks are deservedly one of the most popular garden plants, with their attractive frilled petals, delightful perfume, sturdy growth, and the advantage that their blue-green foliage is a perfect foil to the colour and shape of the bloom.

Above: *Phlox drummondii* is an ideal bedding plant,
liking sun and moisture.

## Echium (ha) Viper's bugloss

A short, bushy-growing plant. The bell-shaped
flowers are prolific, mostly in deep blue, but
there is a mixture of white, pink, lavender, blue
and purple.

## Lobelia (hhp)

Though a perennial, the universal lobelia is best
grown as a half-hardy annual. Very low-
growing, it seldom reaches more than 15cm
(6in). It is a great favourite, and its appearance
in partnership with alyssum marks the start of
the spring and summer display in thousands of
gardens. It is mainly purplish or blue, but there
are some red and white versions. Use in
borders, on rocks, in walls, or hanging or
trailing from baskets. One perennial strain rises
to approximately 1·5m (5ft) so be careful which
you choose!

## Marigold (hha)

See *Tagetes*.

## Mimulus Monkey flower

This is a plant, nominally half-hardy perennial,
which is best treated as a half-hardy annual, and
is excellent for the rock garden where this edges
a pool. Mostly it grows to a height of only
10–15cm (4–6in), though there is at least one
taller variety. It is also known as the musk
flower, but has long since lost its famous scent
and consequently is not now so popular as it
once was. Nevertheless, it shows an abundance
of tiny antirrhinum-like flowers, and is well
worth a place.

## Myosotis (hb) Forget-me-not

The ideal accompaniment for almost every
spring flower or bulb. Its dreamy, wispy, tiny
blue flowers are seen as though through a haze,
and this 'shyness' is the perfect foil to the strong
colours of some of the other border plants. Mix
it with marigolds or wallflowers or interplant
with tulips, half close your eyes, and it would
not be difficult to imagine them as ships sailing
on a calm sea of blue.

## Nemesia (hha)

If you want a massively impressive dwarf bed of
just one plant showing almost every colour
there is, this is the one to choose. The Carnival
Mixture is famous, but nemesia is also available
in a number of individual colours.

## Pansy (hhp)

See *Viola*.

## Phlox (hha)

*P. drummondii* is one of our most popular bedding plants, and understandably so. It packs a mass of colour into a low-growing flower stem, is quick to germinate and remains in sweetly scented flower a long time. The seeds come in mixtures; fill a window box with them and you will have a wonderful perfumed view from that window all through the latter half of summer. Most of them grow to no more than 25cm (10in) but there is one strain that grows to about 40cm (16in) and is excellent for cutting. (See also page 84.)

## Verbena (hha)

This was a favourite of the Victorians and Edwardians: a delicate-looking little plant that is nevertheless remarkably robust, even in poor weather.

Although grown as an annual, for propagation purposes it is best treated as a perennial by taking cuttings, as it is not very good at reproducing true from seed. Low-growing, excellent for edging or boxes (again, there is a perennial version growing much taller and making excellent cut flowers). The white eye serves to accentuate the brilliant colours in which verbena is obtainable – yellow, gold, pink, blue, scarlet and purple.

A very old favourite, fairly difficult to get (but also easy to propagate from cuttings) is lemon verbena, which, although a member of the family, is a shrub or pot plant for the greenhouse or a warm room and is known as *Lippia citriodora*. On its own the plant has very little perfume, but brush against it or squeeze one of its pale green leaves and you are enveloped in a delicious lemony perfume that makes the taste buds work overtime. Keep it free from frost and it will 'perform' for you at Christmas.

## Viola (hhp) Viola and Pansy

This is yet another of the many perennials that are mainly used as annuals or biennials. Most are low-growing, seldom above 20cm (8in). Few people can resist the quaintly marked frilled-edge petals of the pansies, their faces looking not unlike a cheerful little pug dog. They have the common factor of a yellow eye and a generally violet shading around it, but this colour is in turn affected by the other shades – yellow, rose, pink or purple – on the same petal. Some are scented, but in this they cannot match the specialist of the family, the sweet violet, *Viola odorata*, which incidentally is a true

perennial and somewhat temperamental as to when or how it will grow.

The viola proper, which can be grown like the pansy, has become somewhat rare in recent years but seems to be heading for a revival. Probably one reason for its lack of popularity is the fact that it does need fairly constant attention. As soon as the flowers start to go to seed they must be removed, for once the plant sets seed it does not bloom again. Although listed as hardy perennial, the viola will flower in the same year if sowing is done by February in a warm greenhouse, so it has the instinctive compulsion of the annual (and its tendencies) to produce as much seed as possible. (See also page 76.)

## *Bedding Plants*
25–60cm (10in–2ft)

## Antirrhinum (hhp)

One of the most widely grown and most accommodating summer bedding plants is the antirrhinum. Technically it is a half-hardy perennial, but judging from the number of boxes of antirrhinums sold every year by nurserymen and garden centres many people use them as annuals. Left to itself it will go on flowering for years: a small clump growing out of my garden wall was there when I acquired it and so far as I am concerned will still be there

The colour formations on pansies give them a most attractive and unusual appearance. They come in a rich variety of colours, and a mass along a border is one of the most cheerful sights in a summer garden. They are best treated as a biennial, and prefer a moist rich soil.

For impatient gardeners
massed annual plants sown
in spring make a fine show
of colour by late summer.

22

Opposite: Lupins, foxgloves and rhododendrons with a flowering shrub border beyond. To the left, an imposing plant of *Sambucus aureus*, golden elder, and in the right foreground a low bush of silver thyme.

Right: Antirrhinums are deservedly popular for their hardiness and range of colour. Nominally perennials, they are widely grown as annuals or biennials. According to variety they grow from 10cm (4 in) to over 1m (3 ft). This apricot shade, 'Délice', is one of the best known varieties.

Below: *Celosia plumosa*, the fiery red-orange cockscomb, also known as Prince of Wales feathers, has rather odd feather-heads of flower. It is a late-summer flowering plant.

long after I leave. It gives me no trouble; on the contrary, it brings pleasure without any effort on my part, so I shall not disturb it.

For practical everyday purposes, then, we can regard the antirrhinum as a bedding plant. Start them early under glass, or buy them in as plants, and you can have them in flower within a few weeks of planting out. They will last until gripped by frost. Though they carry no worthwhile perfume the odd shape of the flower (bunny's mouth is a common name) makes it easy for insects to get at the nectar, so if for no other reason than to encourage bees to the area of whatever trees or other plants you wish to flourish, a bed of antirrhinums nearby is a good investment.

They were once prey to a disfiguring complaint known as rust, but to a large extent this has now been eliminated by the breeders. Nevertheless, as a precaution look out for rust-resistant varieties – the 'Monarch' strain is good for this. Colour? Take your choice, or better still get a mixture, from white, lemon, pink, red, cerise, crimson, orange, bronze and various others within this spectrum. Height is almost the only point you need to watch if planning a bedding scheme. They vary from the 'Pixy' type, 20cm (8in), up to 'Madame Butterfly', 60–90cm (2–3ft).

## Aster (hha)

Everybody's stand-by plant for late summer: the flower-of-all-work that takes over when the brilliant high-sun performers have faded. So well known, and so universally respected, as to beggar description. Like those other members of the daisy family, the chrysanthemums and dahlias, they appear in various shapes and guises. You can have them in close-knit flower forms or what are known as ostrich-plume types, feathery and graceful. Asters will fill any part of the border, or make you a fine box display, in white, yellow, pink, scarlet and blue. You really could not ask for a more flamboyant finale to the season. (See also page 89.)

## Celosia (hha) Cockscomb

If you are looking for an unusual plant to create interest, try the celosia. Its common name gives the clue to its appeal: the flowers have a peculiar crimped formation. There is a wide range of colours – white, cream, yellow, gold, crimson, pink and orange among them. They are nominally a greenhouse annual but can be planted out in a sunny border, where they will do well at the front. Mostly they range up to

Right: The warm-coloured wallflower, *Cheiranthus cheiri*, sown in autumn to bloom in spring, has a distinctive fragrance and blends particularly well with tulips and blue-coloured flowers.

Below: Annual chrysanthemums are very useful plants. Best started in a greenhouse in February or March, and planted out April–May, they will flower from June till October. This one is *C. carinatum tricolor*.

about 30cm (1ft) but there is a giant strain reaching to about 1m (3ft). One version has quite a tall feathery plume of flower with attractive delicate tracery.

**Cheiranthus** (hb) Wallflower

If a biennial can ever be immortal, then the wallflower will qualify. This rather tangy-perfumed border plant has been a favourite for generations, and its hold is as great as ever. It is a true biennial in that you have to plant it out the previous autumn, but it is hardy and will withstand the winter, giving you the bonus of at least showing leaf colour when so much else in the garden is dead. Then, with the coming of spring, it is ready to take its place in the colour parade, and what a wonderful display it gives: yellow, crimson, mahogany-red, purple – all with that inimitable scent.

You can get wallflowers in several varieties, ranging from dwarfs for the front of the border or for rock gardens (there must be thousands of cottages where they are growing out of the garden walls), to plants suitable for the middle of the border which grow to about 45cm (1½ft). They are excellent not only on their own account; mix them with the late spring bulbs, particularly the tulips. Forget-me-nots (myosotis) also make wonderful companions for them.

One word of warning, however. The wallflower is officially known as cheiranthus, and there is another plant with the same name, commonly known as the Siberian wallflower. This is very similar in appearance, and in fairness is an excellent plant, but it lacks the perfume of our old homely wallflower. Nevertheless, it follows on well and will do its duty as a partner for many of the early and mid-summer blooms.

**Chrysanthemum**

Next to the rose, the chrysanthemum is said to be the most widely grown flower in Britain. Certainly a very large number of enthusiastic growers are members of the specialist society. So strong is their hold on their enthusiasts, in fact, that such a person might deem it an insult to his beloved plants to expect them to take their stance among 'lesser breeds' in a border!

Breeding has caused so many complications that there must be thousands of gardeners who are perplexed by the true identity of some of their favourite plants, not only the family but whether they are annuals, biennials, or perennials. Chrysanthemums and dahlias are a case in

point. They are, in fact, very close relatives, sometimes difficult to tell apart. They are members of the daisy family. This has 13,000 'branches', so the range is wide, and includes such favourites as asters, sunflowers, zinnias, rudbeckias, daisies of course, gazanias and the marigolds. All have the common factor of petals (or florets) radiating out from a centre 'button', but there are some members of the family – notably those from the kitchen garden – in which these points are not so apparent, such as the universal lettuce and the Jerusalem artichoke. Even the lowly dandelion is included.

Chrysanthemums themselves fill a long list of roles, from sturdy little hardy annuals for the border, through the large-sized pot plants and the specialist kinds for exhibition to the grand warm-greenhouse types in which one bloom is almost enough in itself to decorate a room. Compare this with the little spray types with dozens (perhaps even hundreds) of blooms growing together and making up a magnificent

Pompon chrysanthemum 'Bronze Fairy'.

27

display, either apparently pouring out of a large pot and down its sides or as a huge 'cushion' by a wall. Or there is the fascination of the tricolor types growing to about 45cm (1½ft) – single-flowered varieties, zoned in different shades of colour in brown, red and yellow rings, all on the same flower.

Chrysanthemum experts frequently observe a rigid routine, following to an exact number of days the various stages of cultivation. For ordinary garden growers, however, the main concern is over the choice between quantity and quality. Let them go their own way and you will get any number of comparatively small blooms on each plant. Stop them, by picking off certain buds as they appear, and you will be rewarded with prize-size blooms, but far fewer of them. (See also page 89.)

## Dahlia

Dahlias grown from seed, officially half-hardy perennials, are sown early and raised as half-hardy annuals to flower the same year until the frosts. By that time they have become tubers, which should be lifted and stored carefully through the winter until Easter. Meanwhile the seedling plants in the popular types – cactus, decorative, pompon, or the so-called dwarfs – (which reach more than 60cm (2ft)) will grow to heights varying from 30 to 120cm (1–4ft). The taller ones should be staked for comfort, for the flowers are heavy and the stems comparatively frail.

As explained, they require a certain amount of care in winter (a good way is to keep the tubers bedded in a box of sand) if you wish them to flower for a second year and onwards, but it is worth remembering that a packet of seed, producing several plants, will cost at worst only the same price you would have to pay for a single tuber a year later.

## Gaillardia (hha)

Still the daisies come! Gaillardia has its own niche, however, as there is a still different flower colour formation to distinguish it from the two previous entries. Again, it is a perennial raised and used as an annual. Again, too, it is mainly in shades of red and yellow, but here there is a fading of a contrasting colour, strong at the centre and merging more with the main colour as it nears the edge of the petals. There is also a variety that is just tipped with a second colour. Given plenty of sunshine, gaillardias thrive in almost any soil, and make a striking cut flower. (See also page 86.)

## Gazania (hha)

This is also related to the previous plants, and is not unlike the gaillardia. The main difference is that the various colourings, instead of being in bands, are more precisely defined and produce a star effect, radiating outwards towards the point of each petal. It can be used as a pot plant.

## Godetia (ha)

The flowers look delicate, but the godetia is one of the sturdiest and most versatile of our border plants. It prefers a sunny position, and a few packets of the different varieties will provide a fine display for several months. The flowers are rather cone-shaped and in a good range of colours: red, lavender, pink and orange. One strain is known – significantly – as azalea-flowered. Blooms are single or double, and plants are 'dwarf' – about 37cm (15in) – or tall, about double that height.

## Helichrysum (hha) Straw flower

To be told that the latest, international award-winning variety is called 'Hot Bikini' may well set the newcomer wondering what on earth this plant is. The 'Hot Bikini' refers to the fiery red colour of this particular variety. The others range in colour from white through different shades of yellow and red. The flowers have an

A dahlia that can easily be grown from seed is the 'Coltness' hybrid, or dwarf bedding dahlia, a compact single-flowered type, very free-flowering from June on. This is 'Coltness Gem', also excellent for cutting.

Opposite: A Victorian-style planting using red salvias and rows of blue lobelia, ageratum and marigolds.

Opposite: Delphiniums, lupins, petunias, antirrhinums and spiraeas in a mass of midsummer colour.

Right: Helichrysum, the straw flower, has a double use. It is a hardy annual, growing to about 40cm (1½ ft), in shades of red, yellow and white, flowering from July. If blooms are cut before fully open they can be dried and become 'everlasting' flowers, suitable for winter arrangements.

Below: A good study in colour contrasts: the lemon-yellow of the calceolaria makes a perfect foil for the purple-blue shades of the heliotrope. Planting these two together is an excellent device for a colourful bedding scheme.

unusual texture that makes them ideal for drying; cut before they are fully open, they will become superb 'everlasting' flowers. There is a perennial version with silver, woolly leaves.

### Heliotrope (hha) Cherry pic
The common name indicates this plant's deepish-purple colour. Tightly packed clusters of scented flowers make this one of the most attractive plants in the border. A further bonus is that it mixes well: imagine it in partnership

with the marigolds – their bright orange and yellow flowers a vivid contrast.

### Lunaria (hb) Honesty
This plant is also sometimes named the moonflower because of the silvery-moon character of the seed pods. The flowers are purple and quite attractive, without being particularly sensational, but the pods make excellent winter decorations and are particularly valuable at Christmas. No trouble to grow, and well worth the space allotted to them.

### Lupinus (ha) Lupin
You need a number of these together to get the best effect, but undoubtedly they are one of the most striking border plants. The 'Pixie' strain, a definite hardy annual, reaches only 30cm (1ft); most of the others, including the famous Russell lupins, range from 60 to 120cm (2 to 4ft). One type, the tree lupin, is scented and can be used as a hedge. (See also page 87.)

### Matthiola (ha) Stock
There are so many plants with a beautiful evening perfume that it is tempting to plan an all-scented bed or border, but I suggest this would defeat its object. Far better to space them out at intervals along the border, or – better still – to station them all round the garden so that there is something different to catch your attention every few yards. Certain it is that you will pause to absorb the delicate fragrance of *M. bicornis*, the night-scented stock. This hardy annual really thrives at the end of a hot summer's day, its beautiful perfume lasting well into the night.

There are other, equally delightful, forms of stock. The ten-week stocks, as you might infer from the name, are best grown as half hardy annuals, started in heat and planted out where they are to bloom. The other two main types, 'Brompton' and 'East Lothian', are really biennials. Sow these late one summer to bloom early the next, and between them your stocks will provide wonderful perfume for several months. Very satisfying, for apart from the rewards they give they ask very little in the way of preliminary care. They don't need a rich soil and appear to thrive on chalk.

With some ten-week stocks (Hansens seed), discard the dark green specimens at an early stage, as these will probably be the less-wanted single flowers. The double-flowered plants, which will give the best results, are invariably lighter green in their early foliage.

# Annuals and Biennials

**Mignonette** (ha)

It is surprising what effects an uninspiring flower can have in its proper element. Here is one of the surprises that delighted our grandfathers, for mignonette has been a favourite for generations. The flowers are not very large, and are usually found in combinations of yellow and white or green and red. But when evening comes, what a transformation! A very distinctive sweet scent pervades the atmosphere. This one can also be grown indoors as a pot plant.

**Nicotiana** (hha) Tobacco plant

The tobacco plant is another wonderful companion that opens and bestows its perfume in the evening. When at rest, its long narrow trumpet-like flower gives no indication of the delights it can offer. There are now some strains that open during the day, the best-known of these being an All-Britain and Fleuroselect

trials winner named 'Crimson Rock' (self-descriptive!).

Nicotiana is a rather peculiar plant in that it is a half-hardy annual that can be used as a perennial, particularly in the greenhouse. Even there, it is supposed to die down around the end of October, as autumn gives place to winter, yet as I write in early January there is a display of white and purple nicotiana blooms 60cm (2ft) high to greet me as I go into my cold greenhouse: presumably the dull daylight and 'protected' temperature make synthetic summer evenings! Alas, the perfume has fled with the summer sun, but I know it will return with the warmer days. This is their second winter of blooming since the seed tray in which they were started was accidentally knocked off the staging, and they flowered where they fell in the border. Half-hardy annuals indeed! To me, they are a constant joy.

Below: The perfume from nicotiana completes the delights of a summer's evening. These evening glories bring an air of peace and contentment after a hard day's work. They are now available in various shades; this is *N. alata* 'Crimson Rock'.

Although they do not like cold wet weather, petunias are nevertheless one of the brightest inhabitants of the garden. A window box or container full of them is a delight; they also bring a fine display of varied colour to the border. According to sowing time, they flower from May till October.

If you have spare space in your greenhouse, leave some for a few nicotianas. And if you can, have a bed of them below your window and leave the window open on a summer's night.

### Nigella (ha) Love-in-a-mist

Love-in-a-mist is so called because of the feathery foliage that envelops its rather pale blue flowers. Again, one that mixes well with the yellows, but there is a good mixture of colours under the name of 'Persian Jewels', including white, pink, red, and mauve.

### Petunia (hha)

No bedding scheme is complete without a petunia patch. The delicate petals, some of them quite large, have an irresistible appeal, and the pastel shades match the delicacy of the fabric of the flower. Most of them grow to about

25cm (10in), but there is a strain only a third of this height. Natural colours come in all the shades of the rainbow, and in addition there is an extremely attractive red and white striped version.

Petunias make a splendid show on a summer's day, but they do not like cold, wet weather. Heavy rain makes them shrivel and mars their beauty, for afterwards you will often find the petals are spotted. Some newer strains, particularly the $F_1$ varieties, have been bred to counter the effects of inclement weather, and there are strong hopes that eventually the traditional gamble with the weather when sowing or planting petunias will be nothing but a memory.

### Rudbeckia (hb)

This is all things to all men: black-eyed Susan, cone flower, or gloriosa daisy. It is also an

blues or crimson, even dark red. At about 60cm (2ft) they bring grandeur to the border from July to September.

### Salvia (hha) Sage

There are so many unsuspected relationships in the plant world that nothing should really surprise us. Nevertheless, I still find it a little hard to reconcile the famous sage of the herb garden with the fiery salvia that makes late summer and early autumn so colourful. There is no reason why the sage-and-onion partnership of the kitchen should not be continued in the flower garden, for the globe-headed flowers of the allium are a branch of the onion family and would make an excellent foil for the salvias. Salvias, best treated as half-hardy annuals, generally grow to between 25 and 45cm (10 and 18in). The reds are the eye-catchers, but there are some excellent blues, notably a new award-winning *S. farinacea* 'Victoria', which flowers from July to October and offers spikes 25cm (10in) long – marvellous for cutting.

### Tagetes (ha and hha) Marigold

I have included under one heading all three types – the French marigolds, dwarf types normally about 20cm (8in); the African marigolds, somewhat taller; and the calendulas, or pot marigolds, which likewise grow to about 60cm (2ft).

A garden cannot lack colour if it has a few marigolds. Their tight petals, invariably in shades of yellow or orange, draw attention from a long way off. So strident are they that they might be thought to be totally unacceptable in any other colour company – yet put them among any blues and you will get an immediate rapport. African and French marigolds are officially known as tagetes; the French types (shorter) usually come into flower first. The calendula (or English, Scotch or pot marigold)

Above: The daisy-like rudbeckia (black-eyed Susan, or cone flower) is very accommodating, for it can be grown as a half-hardy annual or a biennial, and frequently survives as a perennial. They grow up to 1m (3ft) and are mostly yellow or bronze, with a dark centre.

Right: Tagetes can be sown out of doors in May to bloom the same year, but do better if started in low heat in the greenhouse in early spring. This is the dwarf African marigold *T. erecta* 'Gold Galore', growing to 35cm (1ft).

annual, a biennial, or a perennial. Strictly, it is a biennial that makes a fine annual if sown early enough. As one of its colloquial names suggests, it has a dark eye – brown, in fact – with yellow petals. Yellow is an understatement: it comes in golden, bronze, and what one seed firm calls mahogany. It is a really magnificent plant; each flower can be 10cm (4in) or more in diameter. Award-winning Rustic Dwarfs (a comparative term!) grow to about 60cm (2ft). Some are a little smaller, most are up to 90cm (3ft). Rudbeckias make long-lasting cut flowers, and very imposing ones. (See also page 90.)

### Salpiglossis (hha)

Beautifully-veined velvety flowers, trumpet-shaped and opening out to reveal the full beauty of their myriad shades. The throat is often gold or orange, the rest of the petals veined in pinks,

A border in late summer, with white phlox, heleniums, echinops, cosmos and the flat golden flowers of *Achillea* 'Gold Plate'.

Right: Zinnias are described as half-hardy annuals, but try sowing them *in situ* as they do not like being disturbed. Sun- and dry-weather loving, they reach their peak in late summer. The multi-petalled dahlia-like *Z. elegans* 'Envy', with double or semi-double flowers in yellow-green, is a favourite with flower arrangers.

Below: *Cobaea scandens*, the cup-and-saucer plant, is a strong annual climber. The purple-green flowers quickly cover an arch or fence, and it makes a good screen up to 3m (10ft) high.

person to produce a pure white marigold. Although there are reports that the elusive white has been captured, it is likely to be some time yet before this jewel is released.

Closely allied to the tagetes is the dimorphotheca (star of the veldt) a delightful little border plant growing to about 25cm (10in). It loves sunshine and comes into flower very quickly from June onwards. It is a hardy annual and comes in white, pink, gold, yellow and orange.

### Zinnia (hha)

Closely related to the chrysanthemum and dahlia, though the flowers are a little stiffer and are usually single blooms. But there are plenty of varieties in long-lasting colour, which have the additional advantage of keeping well in water when cut. Several varieties in the 'Ruffles' strain, obtainable in pink, scarlet and yellow, have won awards, especially in America. They do not take kindly to disturbance, so once they have been raised to the planting-out stage it is as well to leave them where they are, only thinning if necessary. Mostly they grow to between 45 and 90cm ($1\frac{1}{2}$ and 3ft), but there is a dwarf version running to about 25cm (10in).

## *Back of Border*
Over 60cm (2ft)

### Althaea (hb) Hollyhock

The hollyhock probably vies with sunflowers in inspiring more 'races' among gardeners than any other tall-growing plant. Sow them early enough under glass and you can see bloom the same year, but they are better grown one year and set out to flower the next. They carry enormous spikes of colour and will easily top most fences. (See also page 88.)

### Cobaea scandens (hha) Cup-and-saucer plant

The cup-and-saucer plant is so named because of the peculiar formation of the flower. It is also known as cathedral bells. One of the exotics, it has to be raised in some heat and then planted out, when it will climb rapidly. It carries a host of imposing flowers in green and purple-blue. Allow it up to about 3m (10ft) space and it will be happy and reward you well.

### Convolvulus (ha and hha)

Convolvulus grows rapidly as a hardy annual. A superior type, the morning glory or ipomoea, is a half-hardy annual — well named, as its

is a no-nonsense hardy annual, unlike the others, which prefer some starting warmth.

While it is not strictly true to say there is very little difference in the three types (except that the calendula is cheaper), it needs an experienced eye to tell at a glance which is which. Despite the comparative sameness of their colours — you don't, for instance, get a red or a blue one — they are so universally popular that one big American seed firm has for years been trying to get the marigold adopted as the national flower of the country. The same firm has also been offering a big prize to the first

(usually) blue or purplish-blue flowers come out to greet the sun on a summer's morning and, if the day is hot, are gone by midday or soon after.

## Cosmos (hha)

A beautiful flower growing to 120cm (4ft) on the end of graceful fern-like foliage. It is sometimes called the Mexican aster, but it does not greatly resemble the asters most of us know. It is more like a single-flowered dahlia with an unusual collar effect. One variety, 'Bright Lights', does produce double or semi-double flowers in gold, orange and red, flowering from June onwards for some weeks. Most of the other types are in orange or red shades. A most imposing plant for the border and, naturally, good for cutting.

## Delphinium (hb) Larkspur

Although the larkspur can be treated as an annual, better plants come from treatment as a biennial. Sow outside in March, for flower in July, or sow in August for flower the following June. It will grow to about 1·5m (5ft), but there is also a dwarf version which reaches only 45cm (1½ft). (See also page 88.)

## Digitalis (hb) Foxglove

Strong spikes, growing up to about 1·5m (5ft), are covered by the mass of trumpet-like flowers of the foxglove. There is a smaller variety, known as 'Foxy', that can be grown as a half-hardy annual and comes in cream, white or carmine. A feature of the foxglove is the mottled maroon markings in the throat.

How sunflowers can grow so huge in the space of a few weeks is one of the mysteries and miracles of the garden.
They frequently reach well over 2m (7ft), and their daisy-like golden-yellow flowers are correspondingly magnificent. Naturally, they need a good sunny position to flourish.

Opposite: Not all sweet peas are climbers. One of the newer types, 'Jet Set', is a comparatively short-growing plant, reaching little over 1m (3ft), but producing long-stemmed flowers that are excellent for cutting.

### Helianthus (ha) Sunflower
One of the tall twins for the back of the border (hollyhock, of course, being the other). As its name implies, the sunflower needs plenty of sun. Its huge, yellow, daisy-like flower, with its vast seed centre, is a very familiar sight. Given good weather, it will flower well into autumn. Some will reach as much as 2m (6ft), and there are reports of giants going well above this, but mostly they settle at between 120cm and 2m (4 and 6ft).

### Humulus japonicus (ha) Hop plant
This is a foliage plant, with pale green leaves, splashed white or gold, which has clusters of small flowers. One of the fastest growing of all annual climbers. it will quite easily grow 3–6m (10–20ft) in a season.

### Lathyrus (ha) Sweet pea
Very similar in many respects to the culinary pea, but with a wider (and often perfumed) range of flower colour. The main difference is that the culinary varieties are cultivated for their seed pods; here, the blooms are picked as frequently as possible, to prevent seed pods forming. Although ranked as annuals, many experts say they should be treated as biennials, started the previous year so that well-formed plants are ready for planting out around April. Feed them well for best results and make sure the ground is well prepared and enriched. Dig the foundations months previously and lace liberally with well-decayed manure or compost. The idea is to keep the roots well fed, so that they make plenty of growth and feed the stems, which will easily reach 2m (6ft) or more in length. But don't give them too much nourishment as a lot of nitrogen will create too much leaf, and you want flowers. The secret is to keep them very well watered, with an occasional liquid feed.

If you want a profusion of blooms on long stems you will have to go to some trouble. The best plan is to grow them on the cordon system, in rows. Pinch out all side stems, grow just one stem up a 2m (6ft) stake, and concentrate all the plant's energy into growing a few blooms. Tie the plant in to the stake as it grows; by the time it reaches the top it will still want to keep on growing but by then some of the earlier flowers, nearer the ground, will be over. Untie the stem, lay it along the ground, and re-train it up the adjoining stake, or even the second one along. This way you will gain extra height and length and correspondingly more blooms.

An easier way, but with less spectacular results, is to let them climb up a garden net or thread their way through pea or bean sticks, like the culinary varieties. Either way, keep picking, every morning, and a packet of seed will normally provide more than enough cut blooms. Not all have a sweet perfume, but there are plenty of scented varieties from which to choose. Among the best are 'Carlotta' (red), 'Swan Lake' (white), 'Noel Sutton' (blue), 'Hunter's Moon' (cream) and 'Leamington' (lavender).

A comparatively new strain, 'Knee-hi', grows to about 1m (3ft) so does not need staking. If sown as a biennial the previous autumn it will reach about 1·5m (4½ft). An even newer strain, 'Jet Set', based on 'Knee-hi', is claimed to grow higher, faster and more sturdily.

Mixed delphiniums, roses and phlox, with geraniums in an urn beyond.

# Annuals and Biennials

## Lavatera (ha) Mallow

The mallow is an attractive bushy plant growing to about 120cm (4ft), with large bell-trumpet flowers up to 10cm (4in) across. It takes up quite a lot of room and is fairly slow to germinate, but will produce a fine show of flowers from July to September. Provides excellent cut flowers – if you can bring yourself to cut them. (See also page 86.)

## Thunbergia (hha)

This plant is also sometimes known as black-eyed Susan, like the rudbeckia, but is not otherwise connected. It is a fast climber given the right conditions of shelter and ample sunshine; otherwise it is better kept in a greenhouse or conservatory. The black eye is surrounded by white, yellow or orange petals. It does well if trained up canes and can also be used as a trailing plant or in pots. It grows very fast up to about 120cm (4ft).

## Tropaeolum (ha) Nasturtium

A versatile plant that is edible as well as eye-catching, for the young leaves can be used in salads. Useful for ground cover, it grows from 15 to 30cm (6 to 12in) except for the aptly named 'Tall' variety, which will reach 2m (6ft) or more and is a good climber. Flowers are mostly gold, orange, yellow and scarlet. It tolerates, indeed thrives in, poor soil. In some districts it is prone to attack by blackfly, which are easily disposed of by aerosol.

Another tropaeolum, canary creeper, is an unabashed climber, very well named as its

yellow flowers clinging to a wall closely resemble a swarm of butterflies or flock of canaries at rest. This one is troubled by a green and yellow caterpillar, cunningly camouflaged to make detection difficult, which rapidly strips the foliage and causes a lot of damage. Deal with it quickly if you see them, for they multiply rapidly.

## Foliage Plants

There are some annuals that are not flowering plants, in the generally accepted gardening sense. Their appeal lies in the colour and/or shape of their leaves. Mostly they have insignificant flowers, which for the sake of the appearance of the plant should be nipped off as soon as they form. Obviously they are retained and allowed to set seed if a fresh stock is required.

## Amaranthus (ha)

This is one of the most spectacular foliage plants known. One strain, *A. tricolor splendens* (Joseph's coat), is aptly named, for its green leaves, arranged star fashion, turn to a mixture of crimson and yellow. As it grows to about 1m

Above: Thunbergia (also known as black-eyed Susan) is a rapid climber, given a sheltered sunny spot, and excels on a patio or balcony. It can also be used as a trailing plant, producing a mass of generally yellow flowers with a dark eye.

Left: *Tropaeolum speciosum* is aptly named the flame-thrower, throwing out long darting tongues of flame reaching over 3m (10ft) as a climber or trailing plant. Perhaps surprisingly in view of its 'hot' colouring, it prefers a fairly shaded site.

(3ft) or more you can imagine the spectacular effect it has in a border. Another version, *A. caudatus*, is the famous love-lies-bleeding, producing long tassels of green, crimson, or white – a great favourite with flower arrangers.

### Beta (ha) Beetroot

Beetroot may sound unexciting as a potential decoration, until you think of its dark purple-veined leaves. Ask for seed of *Beta vulgaris* and you will be rewarded with a display of green, yellow and red foliage.

### Borecole (ha) Cabbage

You can get an extremely ornamental cabbage, with fringed foliage in pink, crimson or purple, and one described as white. Other ornamental cabbages have a pink centre and red or white outer leaves. It almost seems a shame to cook them, and in fact they are very useful in flower arrangements.

### Coleus (hhb)

Perhaps the most widely known foliage plant, this is a greenhouse perennial but is often used as a bedding plant outdoors. It throws up spikes with a little blue flower, looking slightly ridiculous yet quite pretty.

### Euphorbia (ha)

Milkweed, spurge, bottlebrush are names applied to various euphorbias. Rather fleshy leaves in differing shades of pale and dark green, veined paler green or white; an excellent mixture of green and yellow foliage in one fairly large plant. At most it will reach only about 120cm (4ft). The name 'milkweed' is somewhat euphemistic. It refers to a whitish milky juice in the stem that can cause irritation, so be careful how you handle the plants. (See also page 81.)

### Molucella (hha) Bells of Ireland

A free-growing foliage plant, up to 1m (3ft), with rather strangely formed spherical-shaped leaves that vary from green to cream. It is good for cutting, makes an attractive foil to more colourful flowers in an arrangement, and dries well for use as decoration through the winter.

### Perilla (hha)

A lesser-known annual grown expressly for the beauty of its foliage, *P. frutescens* is not unlike the coleus: green with pink variations when young, turning to purple-bronze. Perilla grows to about 60cm (2ft) and is well worth using in the border as a dot plant. Some catalogues ignore it, but it will repay any trouble caused in searching for it.

### Ricinus (hha) Castor-oil plant

Dark green stems topped by bronze or purple leaves make this a most handsome foliage plant growing from 60 to 120cm (2 to 4ft). It is adaptable for indoor or outdoor work and can be sown outside in May. It can also be used as a pot plant. Soak the seeds for some hours before using, to help germination. There are tiny flowers, but the attraction is in the foliage. Don't let children eat the seeds: they are poisonous.

### Statice (hha) Sea pink

This doubles as a good border plant in a sunny position but is even more useful as a dried flower. It bears small lavender-like blooms in yellow, pink, mauve and blue.

### Zea rugosa (hha) Sweet corn

Even sweet corn has its colour variations. There is a special ornamental variety that produces cobs ranging from yellow to purple. It is edible and the flavour is said to be as good as the agricultural variety.

Right: Not all the colour in a garden comes from flowers. Some foliage plants provide spectacular displays, and among these the coleus, or stove nettle, is outstanding for its rich variety of leaf colouring. Technically, it is a greenhouse plant, but it is often used very successfully in borders. Here are some of the 'Kimono' strain.

# 2 *Bulbs*

## Versatile storage plants

No enthusiastic gardener would ever seriously accuse bulbs of being the 'awkward squad' of the garden; but when you come to think of it, that is precisely what they are. Most flowers, whether grown from seed or as cuttings, need nurturing and feeding to bring them to their peak. But the fleshy onion-like substance of a bulb, folded in layers over the embryo in the centre, is its built-in store of sugar and starch, providing all the nutriment it needs.

Conversely, when the flowering period is over, the careful gardener will cut back the dying stems of ordinary herbaceous plants, partly for the sake of tidiness and partly to avoid the risk of disease spores settling on the fallen leaves and causing trouble for succeeding crops. Bulbs will stand no such arbitrary treatment. Those decaying leaves are returning their strength to the centre at their base from which will spring next year's flower. Cut them down at your peril, for you immediately cut off the nourishment and your future display will suffer. If you get anything at all from the bulb, it will almost certainly be a half-sized, ill-formed weakling, with all that means in terms of susceptibility to disease.

If you want bulbs, which demand practically no work on your part (other than planting them in suitably prepared ground) to bring you a wonderful display, you have to pay in kind by putting up with bedraggled leaf stalks for some weeks while they retire from the scene at their own pace. If you must have a tidy border immediately, or want to fill the space they have occupied, the best thing you can do is to lift them gently and heel them in in a quiet but out-of-the-way spot to let them finish their life cycle in peace.

Many gardeners, trying to reconcile neatness with knowledge, tie the leaves into some kind of knot, or bend over the necks of their ripening onions. Except for making the ranks look a little less straggly, this does no good at all: unless the

onions have dried right down they will only waste strength trying to return to the vertical. Tying the flower leaves in knots merely serves to strangle the fibres and impede the return flow of goodness to the base.

It may seem odd to start a chapter on bulbs with a stricture on what you must not do to them when they have finished, but this after-treatment is the most important factor in growing them successfully. Dead-head them by all means – that is how the famous Spalding bulb parade and 'battle of flowers' festivals get the millions of blooms required for such gigantic and breath-taking displays. The plant

Opposite: A bulb bed is a good idea for a spring display, for many kinds can be grown together, and when flowering finishes in late spring they can be replaced by bedding plants to carry the display through the summer.

Above: This excellent arrangement contrasts yellow tulips with a tall dark hedge at the back and a low-growing one at the front; and a height-and-colour contrast is provided by low-growing pansies.

must be prevented from wasting its strength forming seed, but at all costs let the leaves run down at their leisure.

Now that your bulbs are guaranteed safe transit, as it were, let us see what they can do for you in return. They will offer you a wider scope of flower than any other type of plant. The spring-flowering ones will give you bloom indoors from Christmas or even earlier, or outside from January through till June. Then the summer-flowering varieties will take over and carry your display through to the frosts, and there are a few sturdy stragglers that will attempt to complete the year for you. Apart from their versatility in filling bowls, tubs and window boxes – or even greenhouses – they are highly adaptable for planting schemes in beds, borders, rockeries, interplanting with evergreens and other flowering shrubs and plants, for wild and woodland gardens, or for naturalizing in grass.

Nor is this all: they flower in all colours and at all heights. They will provide you with clouds of beauty to be admired *en masse*, or with huge individual blooms, like the amaryllis, that are best admired individually and at close range. All you need is the room to place them and the time to stop and stare as they unfold their beauty and, when that is finished, to treat them reverently!

## Forms of Bulb

'Bulb' is a blanket term covering all bulb-like flower organs: true bulbs, corms, tubers and rhizomes (a few are even known as cloves) sold in a dormant condition. They differ in structure, shape and size, as well as in flowering time, but their function is identical: to tide the plant over its resting period, whether this be in times of winter cold or summer drought.

The bulbous-type plants have a number of categories. Most of them, particularly the spring-flowering ones, bear some resemblance to onions and they are easily recognizable. But the non-expert would have great difficulty in determining the difference between a corm and a tuber or rhizome.

Briefly, a **corm** is the swollen underground stem of a plant with a basal plate from which the roots grow. The **tuber** is also a swollen underground stem, but rounder and more swollen, and lacking the scales that make up bulbs and corms. There is a further subdivision, into **stem tubers**, which have eyes from which the new stem comes (the potato is

Right: Spring flowers in all their glory: tulips, narcissus and grape hyacinths with azaleas and spring foliage behind.

# Bulbs, corms and tubers: planting depths and growing heights

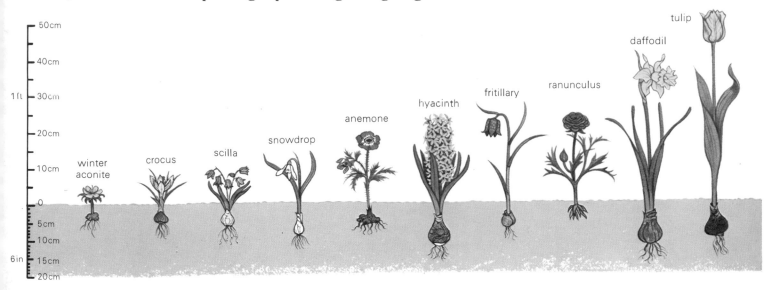

winter aconite · crocus · scilla · snowdrop · anemone · hyacinth · fritillary · ranunculus · daffodil · tulip

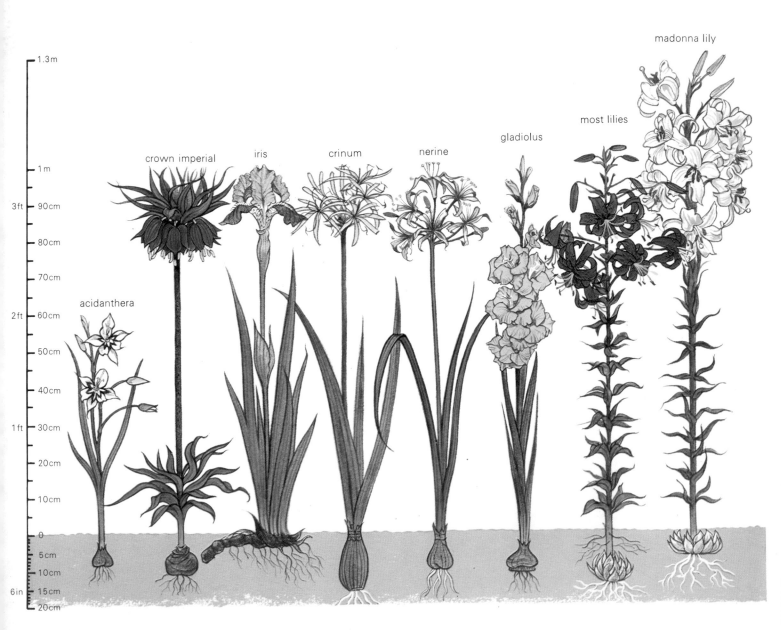

acidanthera · crown imperial · iris · crinum · nerine · gladiolus · most lilies · madonna lily

the best known example), and **root tubers**, which have no eyes and only a bud at the apex – dahlia tubers are perhaps the best known of these types. **Rhizomes** are similar to tubers but more horizontal in shape and with a tendency to sprout new shoots some distance from the parent plant. The bearded iris is a typical example. For the purposes of this chapter we can follow the example of the experts who compile the catalogues and treat them all as bulbs.

All types have common factors: food storage, quick growth under suitable conditions, and the same life-cycle in that during growth and flowering the following year's plant is being formed in miniature. This pattern means that they not only perpetuate the species by reproducing themselves, they usually also produce at least one extra as well. This – or more frequently these – may be smaller and not yet ready for flowering, but will reach the requisite size and strength in a year or two. The flowering thus goes on year after year from the time of purchase, which makes them very good value for money!

With over 4000 varieties of tulips from which to choose, of varying heights, shapes, colours, and flowering times, it is virtually impossible not to get an impressive display. The secret of a successful bed, as shown here, is to mass the various colours.

Right: *Iris reticulata* is a dainty but hardy, winter-flowering iris, ideal for growing on rockeries and in the front of borders.

## Preparation and Care

Gardening with bulbs requires a minimum of effort. Although many should be lifted, dried, cleaned and stored, equally there are many that can be left in the ground year after year, and they will go on increasing in numbers. No other group of plants has such a built-in success guarantee, and so bulbs are invaluable to beginners and to newly formed gardens. Provided they are of flowering size when bought they are virtually certain to bloom the first year after planting. The type of growing medium used is not very important, though some have their preferences for lime or acid soils. It is, however, advisable to enrich the soil if possible before they are planted. Animal manure, if you

Information chart 2 BULBS

### SPRING-FLOWERING BULB CALENDAR (Autumn planted)

| JANUARY | FEBRUARY | MARCH | APRIL | MAY |
|---|---|---|---|---|
| Crocus | *Iris reticulata* | *Anemone blanda* | Anemone ('de Caen' and 'St Brigid') | Allium |
| *Eranthis hyemalis* (Winter aconite) | *Leucojum vernum* (Spring snowflake) | Chionodoxa (Glory of the snow) | *Fritillaria imperalis* (Crown imperial) | Erythronium |
| Galanthus (Snowdrop) | Narcissus ('February Gold' and 'Peeping Tom') | *Iris histrioides* | Hyacinthus (Hyacinth) | Iris |
| | Scilla | Muscari (Grape hyacinth) | Narcissus (Daffodil) | Ixia |
| | *Tulipa biflora* | Narcissus (Daffodil) | Tulipa (Tulip) | *Leucojum aestivum* (Summer snowflake) |
| | | Tulipa (Tulip) | | *Ornithogalum umbellatum* (Star of Bethlehem) |
| | | | | Sparaxis |
| | | | | Tulipa (Tulip) |

### SUMMER-FLOWERING BULB CALENDAR   ✽ IN FLOWER   ♠ WHEN TO PLANT

| NAME | JAN | FEB | MAR | APR | MAY | JUNE | JULY | AUG | SEP | OCT |
|---|---|---|---|---|---|---|---|---|---|---|
| Anemone ('de Caen', 'St Brigid') | | | | | ✽ | ✽ | ✽ | | ✽♠ | |
| Eremerus (Foxtail lily) | | | | ♠ | ✽ | ✽ | ✽ | | ✽♠ | |
| Gladiolus (small flowering) | | | | ♠ | ♠ | ✽ | ✽ | ✽ | | |
| Sparaxis | | | ♠ | ♠ | | ✽ | ✽ | ✽ | | |
| Sprekelia | | | | ♠ | | ✽ | ✽ | ✽ | | |
| Ranunculus | | ♠ | | ♠ | | ✽ | ✽ | ✽ | | |
| Lilium (Lily) | | | ♠ | ♠ | ♠ | ✽ | ✽ | ✽ | ✽ | |
| Ismene | | | | | ♠ | | ✽ | ✽ | | |
| Oxalis | | | | ♠ | ♠ | | ✽ | ✽ | | |
| Tigridia (Peacock tiger flower) | | | | ♠ | ♠ | | ✽ | ✽ | | |
| Agapanthus (African lily) | | | | ♠ | | | ✽ | ✽ | ✽ | |
| Montbretia | | | | ♠ | | | ✽ | ✽ | ✽ | |
| Gladiolus (large flowering) | | | | ♠ | ♠ | ♠ | ✽ | ✽ | ✽ | ✽ |
| Acidanthera | | | | ♠ | ♠ | | | ✽ | ✽ | ✽ |
| Begonia | | | | ♠ | ♠ | | | ✽ | ✽ | ✽ |
| Canna | | | | ♠ | ♠ | | | ✽ | ✽ | |
| Ornithogalum | | | ♠ | | | | | ✽ | ✽ | |
| Colchicum | | | | | | | | ♠✽ | ✽ | ✽ |
| Dahlia | | | | | ♠ | | | ✽ | ✽ | ✽ |
| Freesia | | | | ♠ | ♠ | | | ✽ | ✽ | ✽ |
| Cyclamen | | | | | | | | ✽ | ♠ | |
| Nerine | | | | | | | | ♠ | ✽♠ | ✽ |
| *Amaryllis belladonna* | | | | | ♠ | ♠ | | | ✽ | ✽ |

50

can get it, is by far the best, but never let raw manure make direct contact with the bulb – leave a layer of soil in between. Then a sprinkling of general fertilizer every autumn or spring, lightly raked in, will keep the nutrient 'topped up'.

## Selection

You will naturally want the best bulbs you can get. If you are buying in person and not by mail order, try to select the bulbs yourself, but do be sure not to bruise them.

A bulb in good condition will feel firm and plump, and quite heavy for its size, and there should be no scars. The tunic – the brownish covering – should be intact. Some peeling is not serious, but reject any that have lost a lot of this skin. It is their protection against the depredations of mice and soil-borne infection.

Except for narcissi (which of course include daffodils) bulbs are graded according to their circumference. Normally, the biggest are the best, but it is not always necessary to insist on the top size. The biggest hyacinths will be the best for indoor cultivation, but for ordinary outdoor planting second or bedding size will be adequate. The only other point to bear in mind is that double-nose narcissi will produce better blooms than the round single-nose types.

## Planting

Do not delay planting. Although they may be dormant, bulbs are nevertheless alive and root activity is going on all the time. They are always released for sale at the appropriate time, but if you do have to wait for a week or two, or are planting for succession, store them in a cool dry place and open the bags for ventilation.

For outdoor bedding displays, daffodils and hyacinths should be planted from September onwards, 12–15cm (5–6in) deep and approximately the same distance apart, though they can be closer for a concentrated display or in containers. Tulips should have approximately the same spacing, but the timing is slightly different: they can go in during October and until the frosts. Because tulips are more susceptible than the others to soil-borne diseases avoid, if you can, replanting them in the same spot at less than three-year intervals.

The smaller spring bulbs – snowdrops, crocuses, grape hyacinths – can be planted between September and December, slightly less deep and slightly closer together, say 8cm

(3in) apart. All bulbs should be planted with the pointed end up.

Although most are planted individually, a mass-production technique can be adopted where you are planting in large numbers. Remove the top soil down to planting depth, fork over and loosen what is beneath, set your bulbs in place and replace the top soil, firming in. A little sand beneath the bulbs will help drainage.

Whichever planting technique you adopt, remember that there must not be any air space below the bulb, so the soil must be in close contact all round. Unless it has been raining and the soil is already damp enough, it will be helpful to give the bed a good watering when the job is finished, as the bulbs will need plenty of moisture, without being waterlogged, to get them started.

I have arranged my selection of bulbs into three main groups, according to their flowering time.

## January–March

### Anemone

At about this time we should be seeing the first of the anemones, *A. blanda*, which differs from the normal anemone by resembling a daisy. It is very vigorous, and if left in the ground (tubers can be planted as late as November) will increase rapidly. Given a sunny position, it can continue in flower until April. (See also page 90.)

The colourful anemone can be had in flower in autumn or spring, according to time of planting. Apart from brightening a border, they also make excellent cut flowers, forming an attractive table decoration on their own.

## Crocus

*C. chrysanthus* is one of the earliest bulbs and perhaps the most colourful, for you find it in white, yellow, orange and mauve, and cross breeding has produced various shades in between. It is a strong grower and spreads rapidly. Not surprisingly, it is one of the hardiest of our spring bulbs, and is especially recommended for rockeries and borders. *C. biflorus* is known as the Scotch crocus, because it was first found in Scotland. Its other claim to fame is that it is the biggest of the commonly grown varieties. It is a striking white one, with a yellow throat and purple stripes, and generally flowers from mid-February to March.

There are few finer sights in early spring than crocuses peeping up out of the lawn, and we know they are safe because it is not yet time to cut the grass. Unfortunately, without most of us realizing it, this is the worst possible place to have them, for we are condemning them to a rather short and miserable life, especially if we are proud of the lawn and keep it in first-class condition. Constant pounding by the mower (especially if it has a roller attached) and frequent hosing and sprinkling are marvellous

for the turf but murder to the poor crocuses cowering beneath it all; and additionally they suffer from the rich fertilized soil. Have them in grass by all means, but make it one of the rougher, wilder areas if you can.

## Eranthis hyemalis Winter aconite

This is a long-established favourite, for it has been known for over 400 years. The tiny rhizomes produce a mass of buttercup-like flowers, which frequently appear around Christmas. When they have finished flowering, their leaves provide ground cover until the spring sunshine brings out the later-awakening inhabitants of the garden. They can be left (they will multiply rapidly) but if possible plant them where they will be shaded in summer by shrubs or trees, so as to lessen the risk of the little rhizomes drying out.

## Galanthus Snowdrop

These are obtainable in several varieties, the best known of which are *G. nivalis*, the common snowdrop, which will provide you with an artificial snowfall and *G. elwesii*, which prefers sun and has excellent blue-green foliage as a bonus. Snowdrops also spread rapidly and differ from most other bulbs in that if you have to lift them they should be replanted very quickly – in fact, they are one of the few that can even be lifted and replanted while still in bloom.

## Iris

So vast is the interest in this particular flower that there is not only a national society devoted to it, but there are international associations. The little *I. reticulata*, which appears in several varieties, will flower from January to March. In theory they need a warm sunny position, so how do they manage to flower so early in the year? Another of Nature's miracles and puzzles, especially when you learn that it originated in what we now know as the Middle East oilfields! It is ideal for the rockery, never growing taller than 25cm (10in) and usually a good deal less. Colours are deep purple and gold, and they have a slight scent.

Another in this group, *I. bakeriana*, possibly a little earlier to bloom, grows to only 15cm (6 in) and has main colours of mauve and lilac, with a stronger scent.

A third member of the group, *I. histrioides major*, is another dwarf, mainly blue and scented. It is said to be capable of blooming in January, but I have never been so lucky.

## Leucojum Snowflake

This is another that, if transplanted, should be rehoused as soon as possible. The most widely grown is *L. vernum*, the spring snowflake. Although there are autumn-flowering varieties, these are rather scarce and of comparatively minor importance, for the spring snowflakes are by far the most familiar to our gardeners. Graceful nodding blooms make a pretty sight, with the added advantage that they grow in most soils and most conditions.

## April–June

## Allium

The first of the alliums appears in spring, and what a fine collection there is. There are scores of them, ranging from a few centimetres to nearly a metre in height. All are characterized by a ball of flower on a single stem, and they come in almost any colour you care to name. Many are edible, but here we are concerned with the purely ornamental varieties. They are all hardy, and all very easy to grow. Flowering begins in May or June and, by careful selection of varieties for succession, will go on until autumn. Many make excellent and long-lasting cut flowers.

Opposite above:
A 'spring' bulb that thrives in late summer, *Crocus speciosus* produces its vivid blue flowers in August/September, growing to 10cm (4in).
A peculiarity is that it is sometimes self-seeding.

Opposite below:
Harbinger of spring: *Galanthus nivalis*, the common snowdrop, and one of the most welcome of sights. It grows in a shady spot, and flowers may be either single or double.

Below: The spectacular flag (or tall bearded) irises are universal in May and June, for they thrive in almost any soil, even the poorest.
The colour range is immense; this one is aptly named 'Golden Alps'.

*Erythronium revolutum*
'White Beauty' mixes well
with other small bulbs,
especially in a raised bed
or border.

Right: Spectacular effects
can be achieved in
a hyacinth display by
grouping each colour
separately; the overall
massed effect gives full
value to the range of tints.

undoubtedly they react to soil and position and in general not all that kindly. The real secret is drainage. Sand or gravel will encourage them, but it seems to be a matter of pure chance whether they will take to a shady position, which you might think they would prefer, or a sunny one.

*F. imperialis*, or crown imperial, is the best known and most widely grown in Britain. The flowers are in various shades of red, orange and yellow, but one problem is that the bulbs are very susceptible to damp – hence, partly, the importance of good drainage. They like to be well bedded down, about 20cm (8in) below the surface, and if they survive the spring rains will bring colour and a delicious perfume to the garden in April.

### Hyacinthus Hyacinth

Hyacinths are among the oldest established of all our garden flowers. They were known to the Romans, who grew them for their perfume, and they have been in cultivation in Europe for more than four centuries. They are available in five main shades: pink, red, white, blue and yellow, and there are early, mid- and late-season varieties. There are so many it is best to make your choice from a good catalogue, but among the best known earlies are 'Pink Pearl' and 'Anna Marie' (pink), 'Jan Bos' and 'La Victoire' (red), 'Mme Kruger' (white) and 'Bismarck' (blue). Mid-season favourites include 'Lady Derby' (pink), 'l'Innocence'

One of the tallest is also one of the earliest: *A. aflatunense*, up to 1m (3ft), has lilac flowers in May and June. *A. albopilosum*, violet, also in June, is slightly shorter but marvellous for cutting. Others are *A. cyaneum*, dark blue (June) and good for the rockery, *A. giganteum*, well over 1m (3ft), with violet flowers in July. *A. pulchellum* opens in August and is distinguished by its pyramid-shaped violet flower head.

### Erythronium

So many forms of lily are available that one could easily be forgiven for taking no notice of the lovely May-flowering erythronium. But do try some if you can get them, particularly *E. californicum*, the trout lily. 'White Beauty' is, I think, the best of them all: 30cm (1ft) high, producing several yellow-centred white flowers, turning to lilac as they fade. The leaves are mottled brown.

### Fritillaria

The fritillarias, with their graceful little nodding heads of bloom – some of them not so little, either – will bring perfume and beauty to the garden from April. They are not the cheapest of bulbs to buy, nor the easiest to grow. You could say they are temperamental, for

(white), 'Delft Blue' and 'Myosotis' (blue) and 'Yellow Hammer' (yellow). Later ones are 'Queen of the Pinks' (pink), 'King of the Blues' (blue) and 'City of Haarlem' (yellow). It may be significant that most of those mentioned date from the early days of the century and some ('Lady Derby', 'l'Innocence', 'King of the Blues' and 'Bismarck') are over 100 years old, with 'City of Haarlem' not far behind. No criticism of the modern ones – it is just that these are still such wonderfully good bulbs.

Although they do give such a marvellous display, hyacinths are somewhat temperamental. A light, sandy soil suits them best, and they also prefer a sunny position. But it is the after-care that is the really important factor, unless you want to go to the expense of buying in new bulbs at frequent intervals. Although the bulbs replenish themselves, they will not do so well if left in the ground. Lift them as soon as the leaves have died down, store them in a cool, dry and well ventilated place, and replant them in September or October, pricking over the soil first to ensure that it is loose enough for them to bed in properly. The trick is to ensure that the roots can get a good hold and take in the food required, for hyacinths are deep rooting and do not like being confined.

**Muscari** Grape hyacinth

The great appeal of these plants, to me, is their dwarf stature. I doubt whether they get above 12cm (5in) – and how well they go with primroses and the crocuses. Get a planting of these three and you will have a picture that will keep your memory happy all through the rest of the year. There are many varieties, all predominantly blue, with the characteristic grape-like bunching. Most notable are 'Blue Pearl' and 'Heavenly Blue'.

*M. plumosum* is the one exception to this. It develops curious feather-like filaments (it is called the feather hyacinth), providing a most unusual sight. You may have difficulty in getting it, but it is well worth trying. Because of the 'upturned crinoline' effect, which causes an unusual spread, remember to plant these about double the normal distance apart, so that they do not overcrowd each other.

**Narcissus** Daffodil

Perhaps the big surprise about daffodils is that far more of them are grown in Britain than in the Netherlands, home of the spring bulb industry, and thousands are exported there. The Dutch are actually Britain's biggest foreign customers for daffodils! One of my favourites is

Some bulbs are low-growing and invaluable for introducing a carpet effect. This eye-catching display is a mixture of muscari (grape hyacinth) and *Anemone alpina*.

'Peeping Tom', a bright gold, early-flowering variety that stands about 30cm (1ft) high. Well named indeed, for a spot just in front of or behind a rockery. 'February Gold' is another, slightly smaller, and flowering at the same time. Then there are the sweetly perfumed jonquils – 'Golden Sceptre' and 'Suzy' are excellent varieties here. 'Golden Harvest' is one of the early giants, a big yellow-trumpeted variety standing at about 40cm (16in), and for contrast at this time there is the little white trumpet 'W. R. Milner', only 20cm (8in) high.

Among the mid-season stars are 'King Alfred' and 'Unsurpassable', both about 45cm (1½ft), with yellow trumpets; 'Carlton' and 'Ice Follies' – about the same height – among the large cupped; and *N. poeticus actaea*, one of the pheasant's eye types. Double-flowered varieties come a little later. Among the stalwarts here are 'Texas', with lovely orange cups, and 'Cheerfulness' and 'Yellow Cheerfulness'.

Like most other bulbs, daffodils are very easily grown. They are, of course, hardy, as spring-flowering bulbs must be. They like a well drained soil – dampness is well nigh fatal – but will flourish almost anywhere, with the reservation that acid soil should have a dressing of lime. Plant the Poeticus varieties first; August is about the best month. The others can go in at any time up to mid- or even late

October, while the soil is still warm. You can leave the bulbs in the ground, but divide them after three or four years once the leaves have died down and, unless you have full facilities for drying and storing, replant them as soon as possible.

## Ornithogalum Star of Bethlehem

Like the hyacinth, this is prolific in the number of its varieties. With my soil they take over where the daffodils leave off and last well into June, and I have heard of their lasting even longer, into early autumn in some cases. One thing I have discovered is that they make a graceful table decoration, and they are long lasting in water.

One very popular variety, *O. thrysoides*, is better known as the chincherinchee. This will grow beautifully indoors and proves its use as a cut flower by lasting for three weeks or a month. Unfortunately, it is not hardy out of doors, and needs replenishing every year.

## Tulipa Tulip

The choice of tulips is bewildering, for there are known to be over 4,000 varieties in commerce, increasing all the time, and these are broken down into more than twenty types. The amateur need not worry about all of these, but it will help to remember the flowering periods. Thus the Kaufmannianas (sometimes out in March or early April) and the single and double earlies, generally mid- to late April, are short-stemmed varieties, rarely more than 35cm (14in). At this time also come the Fosterianas, with huge red blooms up to 15cm (6in) across.

The mid-season varieties (early May) are mostly the Mendels, between 35 and 50cm (14 and 20in), and are used for forcing. The big ones arrive in mid-May: the Darwins and Darwin hybrids being the tallest, best known, and probably most weatherproof. They stand over 60cm (2ft) tall. The lily-flowered varieties have pointed blooms, long and narrow. Cottage, or single lates, are mainly large flowered and some have three blooms per stem. The Parrots are easily distinguished by their frilled or scalloped edges. They have a fault in that the stem is weak, so the blooms tend to fall over, but they are excellent for cutting.

Rembrandts and Bizarres have streaks or stripes of colour, and the Greigiis have large, bi-coloured flowers, usually orange and scarlet. The Greigiis have been crossed with Kaufmannianas, and the resultant hybrid is one of the most popular newcomers to the scene.

The petals open out flat when in full bloom, so it is often known as the water-lily tulip. Not my favourite: in my opinion it is a shame that they should look prematurely blown.

Because of the vast list of varieties, of which I think few are household names, I mention none here because I feel it would not mean much. To know the types and their characteristics is the main thing; the varieties themselves are obviously fairly even and I am sure you will not go far wrong whichever you choose.

Tulips differ from other popular bulbs as most of them do not need lifting, but they are susceptible to a fungus disease known as tulip-fire. Affected plants must be lifted and destroyed, and the ground must not be used for tulips for at least three years afterwards.

A more pleasing factor is that tulips go with so many other plants, and especially with other bulbs. Tulips and hyacinths look magnificent together. Tulips can be planted later than daffodils or hyacinths – up to the first frosts – and most of them are hardy, although they relish some protection and prefer a sunny spot. All you really have to do is decide on your planting plan – the colour combinations, for instance – and leave them to get on with it!

The main point to bear in mind is that heights and colours should vary. Get a contrasting colour adjacent if possible, but one that does

Opposite and below: Two of the many types of tulip. Scarlet Darwin tulips (left), with their ramrod-straight stems and severely elegant flowers, are excellent for display. Here they are underplanted with wallflowers.
*T. Kaufmanniana*, the water-lily tulip (below), is shorter-stemmed and has many colour variations on the theme of primrose-carmine-cream.

not clash. A low-growing border plant, for example, makes a good foil to one of the taller daffodils or tulips.

## *June–September*

### Acidanthera

Not many new types of bulb flower reach the amateur gardener, so the acidanthera is worthy of a place in the garden if only on novelty value, though it has been available since the war. At first it was thought to be a form of gladiolus, for its leaves are similar, but the flower is more open and star-shaped – white with a purple throat, and quite strongly scented. Given plenty of sun it will bloom in July, but most of them run from August to September.

### Agapanthus African lily

This is an unusual bulb. It needs rich soil, plenty of water, shelter and a sunny spot, and with all these advantages may still refuse to grow. Curiously, it does much better if kept in a pot. If it favours you, you could get up to thirty flowers per plant. It stands about 60cm (2ft) high and the leaves are evergreen. When it does take, it thrives, and will need dividing from time to time. It has blue flowers, which appear in August.

### Amaryllis belladonna

This is among the last of the summer bulbs to flower. It is somewhat temperamental but wonderful when it does appear. Plant in mid- to late summer, but although it should surface in September it may not appear until the following year. Also, it needs a warm, sheltered spot. It is unusual in that the perfumed pink blooms, on 60cm (2ft) stems, arrive before the leaves, which may continue to survive through winter.

### Anemone

Most anemones will appear now. They need plenty of sun, especially the tuberous varieties. 'St Brigid', 'de Caen' and 'Giant French' are all good and come in a wide range of colours: white, blue, pink, mauve, red and purple. They grow to about 30cm (1ft).

Anemones growing from rhizomes are slightly smaller and are more tolerant of shade. *A. nemorosa* is our native wild anemone. (See also page 51.)

### Begonia

I touched briefly in the previous chapter on the 'double life' of the begonia: the fibrous-rooted types that are better used as annuals and make such fine displays in borders and troughs or vases. Now it is the turn of the tuberous-rooted

Below left: The sweetly-perfumed acidanthera is a comparatively new bulb for summer flowering. Its leaves are like the gladiolus and its growth style is also similar. Delay planting until the soil has warmed; they will reach over 60cm (2ft) in height, with blooms 5cm (2in) across.

Below right: *Agapanthus africanus*, the African lily, is one of the most beautiful plants for growing on chalk. It is late flowering, with glorious blue heads up to 75cm (2½ft) high.

ones. They produce magnificent blooms on slightly ridiculous stems: short, fleshy and also rather weak. Often the weight of the flower snaps the stem, ruining the appearance of the plant. If this happens you can save the situation to some extent by placing the broken flower gently in a saucer of water: your improvised 'water lily' will last for several days. Better still, stake them!

They have done well for me in a sunny situation, but the general advice is to give them some shade. They make excellent solo plants in urns, or can be grouped to form a spectacular three- or five-bulb display. They have a tremendous range of colour: white, all shades of yellow, pink, red and orange. (See also page 18.)

## Canna

This is one of the most handsome of the July-flowering bulbs. It is usually called the canna lily because of the lily-like appearance of its blooms. Rhizomes should be started in pots in the greenhouse in March, and hardened off and planted out in June. Lift them after flowering and replant the following April. This is a little more troublesome than with some bulbous types, but the regal flowers on 1m (3ft) stems make the effort worth while.

Above right: The exotic golden blooms of *Canna indica*, the canna lily.

Below right: Amaryllis, or hippeastrum, is one of the more precious summer-flowering bulbs, fairly expensive to buy, and needing some care if it is to flower out of doors. Placed near a south wall in a sunny spot it should reward its owner with a grand display of lily-like flowers in September. It can be grown in small clumps of three or five, or even singly.

## Colchicum

These bulbs, looking like large crocuses, flower well into autumn. They come in white, mauve and pink, and are so eager to display their colour before the frosts cut everything down that they will bloom for you without even being planted. Set them just as they are on a light window-sill, or even on a mantelpiece, and they will flower without any attention from you.

## Cyclamen

A surprise in August is the appearance of *C. neapolitanum*: it will bloom outdoors till October and still display its graceful ivy-shaped leaves for much of the winter. It can be left in the ground for years, during which time the tuber may grow to about 20cm (8in) across. The pink flowers are pretty, but the leaf display is quite as attractive.

## Dahlia

Kings of the August arrivals are the dahlias — the giants in every sense. They are greedy, for unless they are placed in rich soil they will not prosper fully, and they also need constant watering. Although they are perfectly hardy, you must nurture them well if you want the really spectacular displays of which they are capable. As you know, you can get them from seed for bedding displays, but it is the tubers that will give you the tall ones. Plant them 15cm (6in) deep and don't forget to put in a stout stake. We can get some pretty horrible gales during their flowering period, and unless they are supported your painstaking preparatory work can be ruined in seconds. Incidentally, if you want to cut them, the golden rule is to do it in the morning or evening, never when the sun is at its height. You also have to be careful about lifting them. This should be done immediately after the frost has got them, first cutting the stems down to manageable length.

There are many classifications and hundreds of varieties in commerce, far too many to name here, and new varieties appear every year almost by the score. They are available in most colours, and study of an up-to-date catalogue is obviously the best way of making your choice. I can, however, furnish a quick guide to the types and sizes, which may help in deciding where to look!

Cactus and semi-cactus types have chrysanthemum-style ray florets. Decoratives have flat flower heads with broad, overlapping petals. Pompons or ball dahlias have globular flower heads, and Collarettes have a ring of small petals overlaying larger ones. Large-flowered types are just that: nominally 20–25cm (8–10in) in diameter and 1·5m (5ft) in height. Medium-flowered – 15–20cm (6–8in) and a little shorter. Small-flowered – 10–15cm (4–6in) and normally not more than about 1m (3ft) tall, and Pompons – 5–10cm (2–4in) and also about 1m (3ft) tall.

## Eremurus Foxtail lily

June produces what I regard as one of the loveliest of all bulb-type flowers, which, alas, is by no means as well known as it deserves to be. Another name is desert candle – very apt – and you begin to get an idea of what it looks like, which is reminiscent of a giant hyacinth. It really is a beauty, and two or three grown together in a clump make a majestic display, rising to 2m (6ft) or more. Huge blooms – white, yellow, orange or pink star-shaped flowers in their hundreds – are themselves a good 30cm (1ft) long, and the leaves can be double or treble this. Well-drained and fairly rich soil is essential for their well-being, and so is a good sunny spot. Given that, they will flourish and remain in flower for up to a month. Don't plant them too close together: the crowns should be 60–90cm (2–3ft) apart. If you can bring yourself to cut one of the blooms (and have a room large enough to accommodate it!) it will provide a talking point.

## Freesia

This is one of the post-war miracles, for not long ago it was regarded as almost exclusively for the commercial grower. But new techniques have made it possible for the bulbs to be planted outdoors in the spring to flower around mid-July. Plant about 7cm (3in) deep and the same distance apart. You will get multi-coloured flowers and a spicy perfume till September.

## Gladiolus

Varieties of gladiolus are available in an enormous range of colours, from white through yellow, pink and red to purple. The large-flowered type has majestic blooms on spikes 1·2m (4ft) high. They come in a range of colours. Primulinas are the comparatively small and delicate members of the family, though they will rise to 1m (3ft), and there is a comparatively new strain, half-way between these two, called the Butterfly, differing from them in that the flowers are not hooded. It is advisable to support all gladioli: rather disfiguring for the garden. But wherever you have them remember that they do need sun.

Although August is regarded as the height of the gladiolus season, you can get some to flower in June. These are the small-flowered Nanus types, growing only 60cm (2ft) high at most. They are thus ideal for a border, but use them in groups – five should be the minimum. Plant them in autumn, as though for spring flowering, but protect them as they are not as hardy as the spring-flowering bulbs. They last a long time in bloom, and some throw a second spike.

## Lilium Lily

Lilies are widely regarded as exotic, expensive and difficult to grow. True, they do look opulent and fit only for the hot-house, but they are dreadfully maligned, for many of them are hardy, responsive and trouble-free. Many can be left outside for years on end, and they will produce a grand, even a regal, display every summer.

The lily is as tough as the tulip and less temperamental than the hyacinth, both close relatives. But there is one big difference. Their

'Prelude', a gladiolus with the characteristic bright throat markings of the Butterfly hybrids.

Right: The golden ray lily, *Lilium auratum*, can grow 2m (7ft) high, and flowers in August and September.

Far right: *Lilium speciosum* prefers a rich soil and some shade for its roots. Sweetly perfumed, it flourishes in late summer.

Below: *Lilium tigrinum*, the tiger lily, blooms from June till September.

'bulbs' take several forms. Some, in fact, are not bulbs, but rhizomes or stolons, and those that look more like orthodox bulbs lack the usual 'tunic' of brown skin and are made up of a series of scales. You can propagate by parting these scales and planting them separately, but they must be kept moist at all times. A dry lily is a dead one, for practical purposes. But equally, the lilies you plant must have good drainage. Waterlogging is just as fatal.

Most lilies dislike lime, but the range is so wide that there are a few that thrive in it: *L. candidum* is an outstanding example, and *L. regale*, another favourite, will tolerate lime. Every garden should be capable of carrying a few lilies. If your garden is big enough, or you can provide a large enough area of good well-drained soil, with plenty of humus, you can have a lily display from May till September. Don't lift them at the end of the season unless you have to; the less transplanting they suffer the better.

Some lilies form roots on the stem above the bulb; others root from the base. Stem-rooting ones should be planted 20cm (8in) deep and base-rooting varieties about half this, an exception being *L. candidum*, which need be only 3cm (1in) down. They take up a lot of room, so leave about 30cm (1ft) between each bulb.

You will be tempted to cut some for the house. If you do, cut the stem above the leaves.

As with other bulbs, the leaves are the life blood of the young bulbs forming beneath the soil.

New hybrids are appearing every year, all very attractive. You are certain to get excellent results with them, but don't fall into the trap of thinking you will get wonderful perfume from all of them. Every lily looks wonderful, but not all of them carry noticeable scent. Meanwhile, most of the old favourites will continue to sell well for many years, and you cannot go wrong by growing a selection of the classics.

*L. auratum*, the golden ray lily, produces a number of strongly perfumed blooms, white with crimson and brown spots and the golden ray that gives it its name. It can grow to over 2m (6ft) and flowers in August to September. *L. candidum*, the madonna lily, loves full sun.

It has highly fragrant white flowers in June to July. Height – about 1·5m (4ft). Plant at any time from August till the frosts, but the earlier the better. *L. henryi* gives a spectacular finish to the lily season. Almost the last to bloom, it should go on till late September. This is the beauty with two dozen or more deep orange flowers with black markings, and deliciously fragrant. It is over 2m (6ft), so stake it as you plant.

*L. martagon* is the famous Turk's cap, probably the most widely grown of all. It flourishes anywhere, but seems to prefer lime. Standing just over 1m (3ft), it blooms in June and July with up to a couple of dozen purple-spotted flowers in a range of shades from pink to mauve. There is, however, a catch about this

*Lilium candidum,* the Madonna lily, is one of the best known of the large selection available. It is also one of the comparatively few that thrive on chalk, and can be planted much more shallowly than most – just below the surface. It grows over 1m (3ft) in height, and the fragrant flowers last for about a month in the longest days of summer.

one. It is slightly 'perfumed' – but you may not like it.

*L. regale*, the royal lily, is well named, for it is one of the most accommodating, and best, of all lilies. White trumpet flowers are marked yellow and purple, and there is a lovely scent. It grows almost anywhere, to a height of 1–2m (3–6ft) and blooms in July. Have a clump of these among some ground-cover plants, not merely for effect but for protection for the base.

*L. speciosum* needs rich soil and prefers semi-shade, but will bloom in a sunny spot if surrounded by low-growing companions. Then it will enrich the air with its fragrance in August and September. Not very tall, about 1m (3ft), but with a range of Turk's cap-style flowers and many colours.

*L. tigrinum* is the famous tiger lily. This one has no noticeable scent, but it is a very handsome plant and prolific in bloom, while varieties give succession from June till September.

## Montbretia

This is, in a way, the poor relation of the gladiolus, (they are related, for they both belong to the iris family). They are smaller at about 60cm (2ft), and comparatively restricted in their colour range, being mostly in red, yellow and orange, but you should get two or three spikes from each plant, flowering till September. Try them not only in borders but along the base of shrubs and hedges. They multiply quickly, will soon form a very colourful display and are good for cutting.

## Nerine

Related to the amaryllis and also slightly eccentric. *N. bowdenii*, the easiest and one of the best, needs only shallow planting, but in good soil and in a sunny position. The leaves develop in spring and die in summer without any sign of life from the flower. That comes later, in September, and usually not until the second

One of the 'eccentric' bulbs is the nerine. *N. bowdenii*, the easiest (and one of the best), produces leaves in spring. These die in summer, and the blooms appear towards autumn. Its pink, feathery flowers appear in the second year after planting.

year after planting, when they are pink and feathery. It dislikes being moved, so tickle the soil occasionally to aerate and freshen it.

## Ranunculus

You would expect something special from a plant related to both the anemone and the buttercup, and you get it with the ranunculus. The tuberous rhizome is unusual: six longish claws grip down into the soil. Plant before winter in a sheltered spot, otherwise in February, and the close rosette flowers will appear from June to August.

## Tigridia Peacock tiger flower

This is similar to the gladiolus and in some ways outshines it. The corms are quite small, but they produce flower stems up to 45cm (1½ft), each carrying half a dozen bowl-shaped blooms. Each bloom lasts only a day, but the plants do provide a good succession and there is no noticeable gap in flowering. For best effect use two or three dozen in a clump.

Left: *Lilium regale* stands tall and stately in a border closely planted with annuals nemesia and dianthus and, behind, yellow-flowered *Phlomis fruticosa* and *Alchemilla mollis*.

# 3 Perennials
## Years of colour from seed or cuttings

erennials are the backbone of every small garden. There are probably more of them than of any other kind of garden plant. They are the marathon runners of the herbaceous race. Compared with the sprinters of the annuals and the middle-distance specialists of the biennials, the perennials, sometimes slow to settle down, will go on more or less for ever.

They need not, as might be thought, remain permanently in any particular spot, but are a movable feast of colour and delight, for from time to time they should be lifted or divided and allowed to start all over again in a fresh spot. Their basic advantage over the annuals and biennials is that they do not die at the end of one or two seasons. The flowers will fade and the foliage die down, but if you have done your groundwork properly the roots will remain alive, though dormant, waiting for the spring sunshine to set them on their way again.

Nearly all can be grown from seed. You can also take leaf cuttings, stem cuttings and root cuttings: highly technical sounding operations but fairly simple in fact, given a little enthusiasm and elementary equipment.

Perennials are all things to all gardeners. Some become quite shrubby in appearance. Some suddenly reveal themselves as bulbs, corms or tubers. Some – begonias, for instance – as though uncertain of their function, offer themselves as either fibrous-rooted (that is, they have sensitive hairy roots), which means they can stay in the soil all winter, or as tuberous-rooted. These latter have to be lifted and overwintered in a dry and comparatively warm bed of sand. As if all this isn't enough, some perennials are better grown not as semi-permanent inhabitants of a favourite part of the garden, but as biennials: they are allowed to stay for a year or two and then, as explained, are moved elsewhere.

Most perennials are hardy or half-hardy, and it is interesting that whereas half-hardy annuals

need protection before flowering, half-hardy perennials need protection afterwards. Annuals are dead once they have flowered and seeded; with perennials the post-flowering period is one of rest and recuperation. Cutting down the stems and covering the base is one way of getting them through winter; with some, as with tuberous-rooted dahlias and begonias and chrysanthemum stools, it is advisable to lift and store them in a frost-free place. A dusting of sulphur when they are dry will help protect them against disease.

Some will pay handsomely for a little coddling. Penstemons are a prime example here: they can fall victim to frost and damp, and a useful insurance is to take cuttings (late summer is best for the semi-woody types, when

Above: Delphiniums are among the most spectacular of garden plants and are also among the most accommodating, for they thrive almost anywhere except in damp conditions. Traditionally they are mainly blue, but in recent years new colours have been developed. This bright red hybrid is 'University'.

Opposite: A border planted with weed-suppressing *Stachys lamata* and *Santolina incana*, clipped close to make fat cushions. Beyond are delphiniums, acanthus and white-flowered anaphalis.

| NAME | HEIGHT | | SITUATION | PROPAGATION (Seed, Division, Cuttings) | COLOUR | IN FLOWER | | | | | | | | | | | |
|---|---|---|---|---|---|---|---|---|---|---|---|---|---|---|---|---|---|
| | cm | ft | | | | J | F | M | A | M | J | J | A | S | O | N | D |
| Acanthus (Bear's breeches) | 90 | 3 | sun, part shade | SDC | purple | | | | | | | ❀ | ❀ | ❀ | | | |
| Achillea (Yarrow) | 120 | 4 | sun | D | carmine, yellow | | | | | | ❀ | ❀ | ❀ | ❀ | | | |
| Aconitum (Monk's hood) | 20–180 | 4–6 | part shade, damp | D | blue | | | | | | ❀ | ❀ | ❀ | ❀ | | | |
| Althaea (Hollyhock) | 180 | 6 | sun | SC | lilac, green, blue-green leaves | | | | | | | ❀ | ❀ | | | | |
| Alyssum saxatile | 15 | ½ | sun | SC | yellow, white | | | | | | | ❀ | ❀ | | | | |
| Anchusa | 120–150 | 4–5 | sun | root C | blue | | | | | | | ❀ | ❀ | ❀ | | | |
| Anemone | 30–120 | 1–4 | sun, part shade | D | mixed | | | | | | | | ❀ | ❀ | ❀ | | |
| Aquilegia (Columbine) | 15–90 | ½–3 | part shade, rockery | S | mixed | | | | | | ❀ | ❀ | | | | | |
| Artemesia lactiflora (Wormwood) | 120 | 4 | rich soil, sun | D | white ; silver leaves | | | | | | | | ❀ | ❀ | | | |
| Aruncus (Goat's beard) | 120–180 | 4–6 | part shade, damp | S | cream | | | | | | ❀ | ❀ | | | | | |
| Aster (Michaelmas daisy) | 30–180 | 1–6 | anywhere | SDC | lilac, blue, pink, red | | | | | | | | ❀ | ❀ | ❀ | ❀ | |
| Astilbe | 90 | 3 | shady, damp | SD | deep red, pink, white | | | | | | | ❀ | ❀ | | | | |
| Caltha (Kingcup) | 90 | 3 | shade, waterside | D | yellow | | | | | | ❀ | ❀ | | | | | |
| Campanula (Bellflower) | 30–120 | 1–4 | sun, part shade, rockery | D | mixed | | | | | | | ❀ | ❀ | | | | |
| Carnation (border) | 30–45 | 1–1½ | sun | layer S | mixed | | | | | | | ❀ | ❀ | ❀ | | | |
| Chrysanthemum (Shasta daisy) | 60–90 | 2–3 | sun | DC | white | | | | | | | ❀ | ❀ | | | | |
| Coreopsis (Tickseed) | 30–120 | 1–4 | sun | SD | yellow | | | | | | | ❀ | ❀ | ❀ | | | |
| Cypripedium (Lady's slipper orchid) | 30 | 1 | shade | D | yellow | | | | | | ❀ | ❀ | | | | | |
| Delphinium (Larkspur) | 150 | 5 | light soil, sun | SCD | blue-red | | | | | | | ❀ | ❀ | ❀ | ❀ | | |
| Dicentra | 30 | 1 | sun, part shade | D | pink, purple | | | | | | ❀ | ❀ | | | | | |
| Dictamnus (Burning bush) | 90 | 3 | sun, part shade | D root C | lilac | | | | | | | ❀ | ❀ | ❀ | | | |
| Doronicum (Leopard's bane) | 90 | 3 | slight shade | SD | yellow | | | | ❀ | ❀ | | | | | | | |
| Echinops (Globe thistle) | 60–150 | 2–5 | sun | SD root C | blue | | | | | | | | ❀ | ❀ | ❀ | | |
| Erigeron (Fleabane) | 45 | 1½ | sun | SD | white, pink, lilac, orange | | | | | | ❀ | ❀ | ❀ | | | | |
| Eryngium (Sea holly) | 60–120 | 2–4 | sun | SD root C | blue-green leaves | | | | | | | ❀ | ❀ | | | | |
| Euphorbia (Spurge) | 30–120 | 1–4 | sun, some like shade | SDC | yellow-green, red, white | | | | | | | ❀ | ❀ | ❀ | ❀ | | |
| Gaillardia | 45–90 | 1½–3 | sun | SD | yellow, orange | | | | | | | ❀ | ❀ | ❀ | | | |
| Gentiana (Gentian) | 45 | 1½ | sun, part shade | D (S, but slow germination) | blue, yellow | | | | | ❀ | ❀ | ❀ | ❀ | ❀ | | | |
| Geranium (Cranesbill) | 60 | 2 | sun, part shade | D | blue, pink, red | | | | | | | ❀ | ❀ | ❀ | | | |
| Gerbera (Transvaal daisy) | 45 | 1½ | sun | S | white, yellow, cream, pink, red | | | | | | ❀ | ❀ | ❀ | | | | |
| Geum | 60 | 2 | front of border | SD | yellow, orange, scarlet | | | | | | | ❀ | ❀ | ❀ | ❀ | | |

the wood is young and supple) and overwinter them in a frost-free place.

Most perennials are highly adaptable; only a comparatively few are fussy in their demands as to the kind of soil in which they will grow and prosper. But all will repay some attention before being planted. The patch of soil in which they are placed will be their home for two or three years, perhaps considerably more. Like every other kind of home, it should be made ready for the new inhabitant. The soil's equivalent of a coat of paint is a good dressing of well-matured manure or compost. The plant's roots will feed on that soil, so obviously plenty must be made available for their use from the moment they move in.

Your perennial border is like a long-term investment in the garden. It is not a transient thing so some thought must be given to the project. Don't just rush in and sprinkle a handful of plants wherever the fancy takes you. Think about heights, so that one plant will not be swamped by another; about colour, so that there is no clash, and about flowering succession, so that there are no bare patches. Think, too, about when you wish to plant. In autumn the soil will still be warm and can take young plants raised from seed in spring; in spring, though you must wait for it to warm up, you will have been able to dig over the plot and let the frost break it up, and this timing will be helpful when setting out cuttings taken in

| NAME | HEIGHT | | SITUATION | PROPAGATION (Seed, Division, Cuttings) | COLOUR | IN FLOWER | | | | | | | | | | | |
|---|---|---|---|---|---|---|---|---|---|---|---|---|---|---|---|---|---|
| | cm | ft | | | | J | F | M | A | M | J | J | A | S | O | N | D |
| Gypsophila (Baby's breath) | 30–90 | 1–3 | sun | SC | white, pink | | | | | | | ✽ | ✽ | ✽ | | | |
| Helenium (Sneezeweed) | 45–120 | 1½–4 | sun | SD | orange, crimson, yellow | | | | | | | ✽ | ✽ | ✽ | ✽ | | |
| Helianthus (Sunflower) | 150 | 5 | sun | SD | yellow, gold | | | | | | | | ✽ | ✽ | ✽ | | |
| *Helleborus niger* (Christmas rose) | 15–30 | ½–1 | shade | D | white | ✽ | ✽ | | | | | | | | | | |
| Hemerocallis (Day lily) | 90 | 3 | sun | D | orange, pink, gold, cream | | | | | | | ✽ | ✽ | ✽ | ✽ | ✽ | |
| Hosta (Plantain lily) | 60 | 2 | sun | DC | lilac ; blue-green/ white leaves | | | | | | | ✽ | ✽ | ✽ | | | |
| Hypericum (St John's wort) | 30 | 1 | sun, part shade | SDC | yellow | | | | | | | | | | | | |
| Kniphofia (Red hot poker) | 60–120 | 2–4 | sun | D | red, yellow, white | | | | | | | ✽ | ✽ | ✽ | ✽ | ✽ | |
| Lavatera (Mallow) | 75 | 2½ | sun | SC | pink, white | | | | | | | ✽ | ✽ | ✽ | | | |
| Limonium (Sea lavender) | 30–60 | 1–2 | sun, rockery | S root C | pink, lilac | | | | | | | ✽ | ✽ | ✽ | | | |
| Linum (Flax) | 15–45 | ½–1½ | sun, shelter, rockery | SD | blue, white, pink, red, yellow | | | | | | ✽ | ✽ | ✽ | ✽ | | | |
| Lupinus (Lupin) | 60–150 | 2–5 | sun, part shade | SC | mixed | | | | | | | ✽ | ✽ | | | | |
| Nepeta (Catmint) | 90 | 3 | sun, good in chalk | SC | lilac | | | | | | ✽ | ✽ | ✽ | ✽ | ✽ | | |
| Paeonia (Paeony) | 60–90 | 2–3 | sun, part shade | D | crimson, pink, white, yellow | | | | | | ✽ | ✽ | | | | | |
| Papaver (Oriental poppy) | 60–90 | 2–3 | sun | SD root C | red, orange, white | | | | | | ✽ | ✽ | | | | | |
| Pelargonium | up to 90 | 3 | border or greenhouse | C | red, white, pink, blue | | | | | | ✽ | ✽ | ✽ | ✽ | ✽ | ✽ | |
| Penstemon | 15–60 | ½–2 | sun, part shade, rockery (dwarfs) | DC | pink, lilac | | | | | | | ✽ | ✽ | ✽ | ✽ | | |
| Phlox | 15–60 | ½–2 | dwarfs like sun ; others part shade | D | mixed | | | | | | | ✽ | ✽ | ✽ | ✽ | | |
| Potentilla (Cinquefoil) | 15–60 | ½–2 | sun, rockery (dwarfs) | D every 3–4 years | red, orange, yellow, white | | | | | | | ✽ | ✽ | ✽ | ✽ | | |
| Primula (Primrose, Polyanthus) | 7.5–60 | ¼–2 | part shade | SD | mixed | | | | ✽ | ✽ | ✽ | | | | | | |
| *Primula denticulata* | 30 | 1 | sun | SD | white, pink, lavender | | | | | | ✽ | ✽ | | | | | |
| Rheum (Rhubarb) | 180 | 6 | shade, damp | D | deep red | | | | | | ✽ | | | | | | |
| Rudbeckia (Cone flower) | up to 120 | 4 | sun | D | yellow, red, bronze | | | | | | | ✽ | ✽ | ✽ | ✽ | | |
| Saxifrage (Rockfoil) | 7.5–30 | ¼–1 | sun, rockery | SDC | pink | | | | | | ✽ | ✽ | ✽ | ✽ | | | |
| Scabiosa (Scabious) | 60 | 2 | sun | D every 3 years | blue, white, pink | | | | | | | ✽ | ✽ | ✽ | ✽ | | |
| Stachys | 30 | 1 | sun | D | grey leaves | | | | | | ✽ | ✽ | ✽ | ✽ | | | |
| Vinca (Periwinkle) | 15–60 | ½–2 | sun | D or layering | blue, red, white | | | | | | | ✽ | ✽ | ✽ | ✽ | ✽ | |
| Viola | 7.5–22.5 | ¼–¾ | part shade | S | mixed | | | | | | | ✽ | ✽ | ✽ | ✽ | ✽ | |
| Yucca | 150 | 5 | sun | root C | white | | | | | | | | ✽ | ✽ | ✽ | ✽ | |

autumn and sheltered through winter. Either way, try to ensure that any manure you dig in is well seasoned.

Having made certain that the soil is in good condition to receive your plants, you must help it to hold them. When you plant, firm the soil thoroughly. Tread it down hard, so that it can grip round the stems and roots. And remember that it is *your* border. Visiting experts may look down their noses at your choice and placings: disregard them. Beauty is in the eye of the beholder here as much as anywhere. Only if you are not satisfied is there something wrong, and the great blessing about a herbaceous border is that you can change it as much as you like next year.

*Potentilla fruticosa mandshurica*: potentillas are excellent for shrubberies in small gardens, with their sage, silver- or grey-green leaves and abundant, brightly-coloured flowers.

# Inside the perennial

Perennial blooms vary enormously in colour, form and size, but they all share the same basic parts. Sepals protect the growing bud, until the petals open to reveal the male and female organs inside. When pollen is carried from the anther (male) to the stigma (female) germination takes place and a seed is formed.

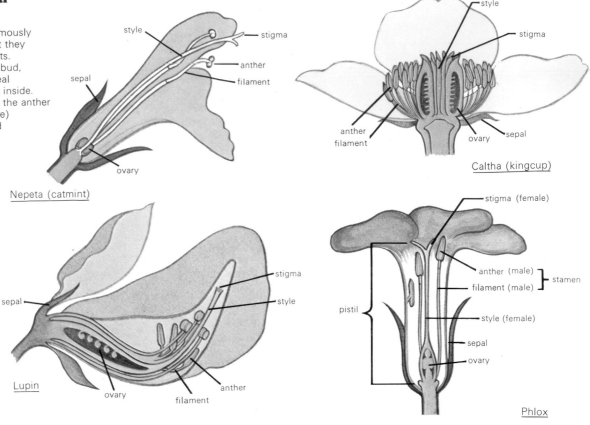

Nepeta (catmint)

Caltha (kingcup)

Lupin

Phlox

There are a few standard practices. Naturally, to avoid masking you will put the small plants at the front or edge, building up towards the centre and back. A practical point to bear in mind is that tall plants can easily be knocked down by wind and rain. Staking them is laborious but an insurance; if you want to avoid this trouble, keep your plants at a maximum height of around 1m (3ft).

Perennials will give you colour, whether of foliage or flowers, through the greater part of the year. But they will not all do that at the same time, nor will they do it for the same consistent periods. Some flower early, others late. Some bloom for many weeks, others for a few days or even hours, so plan a succession, arranging your planting in such a way that as one plant goes over its neighbours immediately surrounding it are coming up to their best.

This leads us to the key factor in planning a perennial border (which, of course, can also include annuals). Make it a good bold one, not a straggly line of plants skirting the edge of a path, where every leaf is under the eye. If you can spare a width of two metres out from the back fence, use it all. True, you won't be able to reach this far from the front comfortably if you wish

to hoe or rake, but you should not have much to do once the plants are growing well: few weeds will have the chance to handicap your plants and embarrass you.

One way to achieve depth and give the plants room to breathe is to have a bed in the middle of the lawn. We have rose beds, so why not other types? It will be like a floral island, and in this case your taller plants will be in the middle.

Drainage is another important item. Except for the specialist bog plants, few perennials relish wet feet. Heavy moisture-holding clay can be alleviated to some extent with a layer of gravel, sand or peat; easily drained light sand can be given body with a good layer of straw manure or compost or, again, of peat, but bear in mind that peat is acid and could upset the chemical balance of your soil and what grows in it.

When preparing a new bed, it is a common practice to plant potatoes there for the first year, to clean the soil. If you should be troubled with bindweed, put in zonal pelargoniums instead: they are more decorative and bring a touch of poetic justice by strangling the strangler yet without affecting any other plant.

The object of the herbaceous or perennial

Opposite: Himalayan primulas and tall, luxuriant plants of the Himalayan poppy, meconopsis, with its flowers in many shades of blue, combine to make a colourful summer display.

72

Above: Pelargoniums have attractive foliage as well as flowers, and a distinctive but attractive scent. The 'zonal' colourings on the leaves are more clearly marked in some varieties than in others. Here is 'Mrs Henry Cox'.

Opposite above: *Helleborus niger*, the Christmas rose, whose delicate white flowers are a pleasing sight in the depths of winter.

Opposite below: An unusual greenhouse primula, *Primula sinensis* 'Dazzler', which has long been cultivated in China, yet has never been found growing wild anywhere in the world.

smothered and hidden by the younger and more boisterous inhabitants.

You will get few, if any, tall plants in flower much before Midsummer's Day, and indeed very few are listed in my TALL selections. Blame this on me for an arbitrary decision: I don't regard a plant as tall unless an ordinary-sized human can look it straight in the eye.

## January–March

### SHORT

**Gentiana** Gentian
According to the catalogues, gentians flower from March to August. True, they do, given the proper circumstances. But your March flower will come from the exquisite little *G. excisa*, perhaps the most popular of all the gentians, which often endears itself doubly by thrusting its lovely blue trumpets out of the soil again in autumn. Contrast this with *G. freyniana*, a paler blue that probably will not show until August but will then go on until September.

And if you thought that gentians must be blue and small, there is a 'black sheep' – though a very pleasing one – called *G. lutea*, which appears in the height of summer and is not only yellow but an outsize yellow, standing a comfortable 120cm (4ft), and almost qualifying for a place at the back of the border or in the centre of an island bed.

**Helleborus** Christmas and Lenten rose
Here is another early spring flower that doesn't know when it is supposed to stop. The most famous of the family, *H. niger*, is the fabulous Christmas rose, which sometimes really is out at Christmas and beats the snowdrops as the first messengers of spring. There's something of a misnomer here for *niger* means black, yet the flowers are pure white, with yellow centres.

Although I love it, I feel the Christmas rose is somewhat overrated. Appropriately enough, if it is to be part of the Christmas celebrations, it demands a rich diet, but even then does not always deign to flower. (Incidentally, the helleborus is not a very sociable plant. The Greeks named it 'the food that kills'; it is in fact slightly poisonous, so don't let a young child eat any part of it.)

The Lenten rose, *H. orientalis*, almost equally popular, appears around January and may go on until March. It is a little taller – about 45cm (1½ft) high – and comes in white, crimson or purple.

border is to maintain a good show of colour for as long as possible, so it will simplify the choice of plants to list them month by month and subdivide each list into SHORT – up to approximately 60cm (2ft), MEDIUM – 60–150cm (2–5ft) and TALL – over 1·5m (5ft).

Because conditions of soil, climate, cultivation technique and even quality of seed or plant vary so widely, it is impossible to state categorically exactly when a plant will bloom, or its exact height. So the details that follow may well be a few centimetres or a couple of weeks adrift either way. This is intended only as a rule-of-thumb guide in planning your programme of succession. The flowering periods given are the assumed limit over which that particular plant will flourish. It does not necessarily mean that one single bloom will last for months on end: you may have to get a succession of varieties, and proper study is best done with the aid of a good nurseryman's catalogue.

Most perennials reach their peak around May–June, obligingly coinciding with the time when the spring bulbs are looking depressingly drab and dead yet you dare not touch them. Your early perennials will do a lot to hide these gaps and in their turn, as they fade, will be

Less well known but equally spectacular is *H. corsicus*. This produces bright green cup-like flowers from January until April or later, and then continues with a display of large blue-green stems which, as winter approaches, splay out as the new shoots force their way through. Quite an extraordinary plant.

**Primula** Primrose

These provide one of the big cross-sections of plant life that tend to baffle the tidy gardener who would like all his subjects neatly pigeon-holed. There are dwarf kinds, preferring some shade, and most of them partial to peaty soil. There are moisture loving kinds, growing up to 90cm (3ft) that thrive in moist soil and make a waterside look colourful. Other members of the family are equally well known as primroses and polyanthus. The cultivated primroses, while retaining the shape and, in some cases, approximately the deep yellow-cream colour of the wild primroses, come in a wide range of colours – gold, various shades of red and even blue.

One of the earliest and best known, *P. denticulata*, the drumstick primula, brings early colour to the rock garden with globular masses of flowers in white, rose or lavender. A

word of warning: although they are recognized as rock plants, do not subject primulas to the full glare of the springtime sun. For they are also waterside plants, liking some shade. They should flower from March to May but will do so only if you keep them well provided with water.

## MEDIUM

**Caltha** Marsh marigold; Kingcup
This plant will bring a sunburst of colour to the edge of a pool for a couple of months from March onwards. Most flourish up to a height of 60cm (2ft) or more but there are some dwarfs. One, *C. alba*, is a white form growing to only 15cm (6in). A pool edge is not essential for these early plants: a dampish shady area will suit them admirably.

## *April*

### SHORT

**Alyssum**
Another prime example of a complicated plant that can be either annual or perennial. It is a

great favourite in the border – its classic partnership with lobelia has already been mentioned – and it also goes well with aubrietia. The best known, *A. saxatile* (gold dust is the aptly descriptive common name), which comes in a number of varieties, is sown from February to May in a greenhouse or frame, or outdoors in June or July, to flower the following spring from April to June. Following that its flowers, mainly yellow, will continue to appear for many years.

But there are other varieties of alyssum which will flower for a longer period. *A. argenteum*, for instance, will go on until August and will give a good showing of grey or silver foliage as well. There is even a shrubby version, *A. spinosum*, with pink and white flowers, lasting until August. (See also page 18.)

**Doronicum** Leopard's bane
This is a glorious yellow daisy-like flower like a cross between a chrysanthemum and a dandelion. There is not a great deal of it in height – say 30cm (1ft) – but its blast of tightly-packed golden-yellow petals will cheer you up well into late spring and early summer. If cut back after flowering, it may produce a second show in autumn.

**Viola**
An old favourite that has a sentimental appeal. It is coming back into popular esteem now, after a period in the doldrums. Whether this was because of its own idiosyncracies or due to the modern human desire not to do much maintenance work is hard to say. The fact is that if you want violas to go on blooming for the many months of which they are capable you have to prevent them making seed. This is done very simply by removing the flowers when they are finished and are settling down to produce the next generation. If you remove the fading blooms the viola will try to outdo you by producing more flowers, which, if left to themselves, would likewise produce more seed.

Whichever way you choose to play it, you are bound to win, for whether you allow them a long or short life the violas will always put their heart into providing you with the finest display they can manage. They will flower from April onwards, mostly until June, but there is at least one variety, *V. martin*, that will go on until August. Mostly, all they ask is a good loamy soil and a fairly cool position.

And don't think they are all violet in colour. 'Bowles Black' is one of the nearest approaches

The marsh marigold, or kingcup, is ideal for a damp border or edge of a pond, growing to 60cm (2ft), and bringing a touch of golden colour in March and April.

yet to this satanic ideal that has such a fascination for plant breeders: a rich velvety purple-blue. In complete contrast there is *V. alba*, pure white, and you can have yellow or pinks as well. Bear in mind how closely allied they are to the pansy, and you see the colour possibilities. The variety most famous for perfume is *V. odorata*, the sweet violet, which grows about 15cm (6in) high. Few exceed 25cm (10in). (See also page 21.)

## MEDIUM

### Dicentra

This plant has dainty, feathery foliage and unusual pendant flowers. *D. spectabilis* (bleeding heart) in particular has beautiful foliage and large, heart-shaped, rosy-pink flowers with white tips. *D. eximia* has grey-green leaves and rosy-purple flowers, and makes a good edging plant. Neither is likely to grow much above 45cm (1½ft), flowering from April or May through to June or July, and possibly August.

## *May*

May is really the month when the perennials begin to take charge of the flower garden. You can, believe it or not, even have an orchid blooming in the border then!

## SHORT

### Cypripedium Lady's slipper orchid

This is quite an amenable plant, small but hardy, and by no means the heated greenhouse aristocrat many people still seem to expect it to be. You may have some difficulty in getting one – it is a specialist subject – but it will not present any real difficulties provided you can keep it in a cool, fairly damp site. This is one of the comparatively few plants that relish a north-facing situation. Potted up in winter and kept indoors in a cool but not draughty spot, it could bloom very early in the year. Expect it to flower until June. It will grow to about 30cm (1ft).

### Dianthus

The perennial dianthus, covering varieties of sweet williams, pinks and carnations, are dealt with in a similar way to the annual version: used with care and determination you can have a continual source of that delightful sweet clovey scent from April to September or October. (See also page 19 and page 90.)

Left: The 'sunburst' of golden flowers – about 6cm (2½in) across – of the doronicum (leopard's bane) provides an early splash of colour in a border. It is also good as a cut flower.

Below: The sweetly-scented scarlet *Viola × wittrockiana* is one of the most flamboyant and attractive of all the garden pansies.

*Gerbera jamesonii*
produces colourful flowers
well into autumn.

### Erigeron Fleabane
This has daisy-like flowers, mostly under 30cm (1ft), and will provide a successional range of colour all summer in white, pink, lavender, orange and mauve. It is very similar in appearance to the aster. Erigeron thrives on sandy soil but will accept any home that is fairly dry and sunny. It spreads rather quickly, so when planting leave at least 30cm (1ft) space between. It is advisable to divide clumps every second or third year.

### Gerbera Transvaal daisy
This is a little larger than the fleabane. It needs a sunny position and is rather tender, so should be lifted and taken into a shed or cool greenhouse for the winter. The *G. jamesonii* hybrids produce a fine range of yellow-centred flowers in white, yellow, cream, pink and red, providing a grand collection of cut flowers all through the summer. They are easily raised from seed sown in February in a warm greenhouse, and are well worth the slight trouble they cause in raising.

### Limonium Sea lavender
The common name gives the clue as to the type of plant this is. It grows up to 60cm (2ft) high and has tiny pink- or lavender-coloured flowers. It can be started from seed but this is a long process, taking up to three or even four years. Excellent for seaside gardens as it seems to thrive on salt air.

### Linum Flax
The common name immediately conjures up visions of a pretty little blue flower. But lurking under its official name are a host of other colours. The perennial versions come in yellow, white and pink as well as blue, and additionally

Right: *Linum narbonense* 'Heavenly Blue' bears a mass of traditional flax-blue flowers from mid-summer to late autumn.

there are some annual varieties, slightly shorter, in vivid red or scarlet. Be careful also that you place your flax in a sunny position. Near the front of a south-facing rock garden is ideal for the flax will hide its face if it is in shade. But if the sun lasts until September, the linum will stay with it.

The flowers may last only one day, but if you are prepared to dead-head them frequently you will get a continuous supply of bloom. *L. aureum*, as its name indicates, is a golden colour, and grows taller than the rest.

### Potentilla Cinquefoil
This is one of the most obliging plants in the herbaceous range. Most are ideal for the rock garden, flowering in dry, sunny conditions from April or May to September, in shades of scarlet, pink, yellow, orange and sundry tints in between. Usually they are less than 30cm (1ft) in height. There are shrubby versions available, but the herbaceous types offer the greater variety of choice and flower. One of the most popular is 'Gibson's Scarlet', which offers the additional attraction of strawberry-like leaves. This is an old variety that regained its popularity only a few years ago and now seems set for a period of prosperity. 'Miss Willmott', a little taller, is also red. A golden beauty that will shine from the front of the rockery is *P. aurea*, which will flower for a couple of months from May onwards. (See also page 121.)

## Saxifraga Rockfoil

Yet another front-of-border plant that makes rock gardens worth having. The best known variety is probably 'London Pride', usually (though not quite accurately) listed as *S. umbrosa*. Pink flowers in a nest of purplish stems make it an unforgettable sight, which no doubt largely accounts for its popularity. In truth it is rather invasive and does need keeping in check. Very tough, it will flower right through summer into autumn.

## Sedum Stonecrop

A particularly interesting, even entertaining, plant. As the common name indicates, it does bear some slight resemblance to gravel, but the colours of the leaves and flowers make it a very colourful gravel. Sedums rank among the succulents and are widely regarded as plants to decorate the rock garden, but they can have a striking effect at the front of a border. On the whole, they are very short-stemmed. The maximum height is about 30cm (1ft), with the majority barely half this, or even less. They like a sunny position and one of their attractions is the way butterflies flutter around them. Very good for ground cover, the flowers are mostly orange and red but there are some blues and greys. They will provide bloom until October.

## Stachys

A sun-loving plant with several varieties, the best known of which is 'Silver Carpet', a grey-foliage plant, ideal for the front of the border, and indeed one of the best of the foliage plants. It is evergreen and makes a perfect contrast to other plants in the border. This one is purely foliage and does not flower but there are other varieties having pink or red flowers, which will last easily until August.

## MEDIUM

## Aquilegia Columbine

This is a versatile member of the buttercup family, and in its various guises will flower from

Potentilla, or cinquefoil, is a member of the rose family and flowers almost continuously from early summer to late autumn. *P. atrosanguinea* 'William Rollinson' (sometimes called 'Rollison'), shown here, is a semi-double vermilion and yellow, growing to 60cm (2ft). It likes full sun.

A mixed border closely planted to suppress weeds. Plants include
blue campanulas and golden heliopsis.

## Perennials

May till October. The flowers vary from little alpines to tallish, elegant, star-shaped blooms and are ideal for cutting. They prefer some shade but are quite accommodating as to where they live. The dragonfly hybrids are renowned for their colour varieties – red, yellow and copper – which usually bloom from May to July. Follow them with another strain, the McKana hybrids, which have a blue tinge among their colour range, and you will have colour into August or September.

### Euphorbia

A very colourful plant, though it does not have real flowers, but bracts, which are coloured leaves on a flower stalk. Invariably the flowers themselves are insignificant. Most are yellowish green, but there are exceptions. The aptly named 'Fireglow' is a striking orange-red. Given good conditions, some will show their colour in April, but they are at their best from May till July. The poinsettia is the best known euphorbia, though it is not regarded as an outdoor plant in Britain. (See also page 42.)

### Hemerocallis Day lily

This name means, in approximate terms, 'beautiful for a day' – extremely apt, for there are few plants that can beat the day lily for beauty of flower. While it is true the individual blooms are usually over in a single day, they manage to arrange such a fine succession that you do not notice. They always appear beautiful and fresh, as indeed they are. These plants are truly perennial in the sense that a clump will last more or less for ever. I once had some that were reputed to have been in position for over twenty years undisturbed. They had been planted at the front of a shrubbery that had become overgrown, and understandably they were rather thin and spindly. But they did produce a mass of lovely orange colour, which looked wonderful with the sun shining on them through the leaves of the surrounding shrubs, and I loved them. Nowadays you don't have to be content with orange as the exclusive shade, as they come in tones of pink, gold and even cream. As for their 'day', it is quite a long time: between them they will keep you in colour from May till the end of September.

### Kniphofia Red hot poker; Torch lily

This is not a very elegant plant on its own, but is certainly distinctive with its long upright stem of brightly coloured flowers. These are principally red, of course, but are also now

Above: Euphorbias (spurges) are mainly fast-growing plants. The greenish yellow 'flowers' of *E. wulfenii* 'Lambrook Gold' appear in April and last for some weeks until the blue-green foliage takes over.

Below: The red hot poker, kniphofia or tritoma, one of the hardiest of border perennials. The bright flower spikes grow to 1m (3ft) or more and are long lasting.

Paeonies are either herbaceous or shrubby perennials, according to variety. All are magnificent in bloom and mostly hardy, though they do not like being disturbed. This excellent double-flowered crimson border variety is *P. officinalis rubraplena*.

available in yellow and white, and there are experiments with green shades. I like to see them amid a collection of ornamental grasses; the stark brightness contrasts with the subtle tones and quiet grace of the grasses to make a pleasing and strangely restful effect, but they can also be used 'architecturally' in a general bed or border.

## Paeony

Here we have one of the aristocrats – not to say autocrats – of the garden. The paeony can be either a herbaceous perennial or a shrubby one. The main difference is that you propagate the first by division (not easy, as the roots are very tough) and the second by layering. Spring or autumn is the time. They will take at least four years before they look anything like the type of plant you expect to see, and they resent being moved. But leave them to show themselves in their own good time and they will repay your patience.

It pays to give them a richly manured bed – they will expect to be drawing nourishment from it for a good many years. Mostly they are a purplish red. 'Bowl of Beauty' is probably the best known, and it does carry some perfume. There are some white and yellow varieties, which also enrich the air with their scent. The rather tight flowers last well when cut, and are especially effective in a table decoration.

## Papaver Poppy

Poppies are in a sense the big, blousy, lovable trollops of the border – and that is not meant disparagingly. The paper-thin blooms are certainly spectacular. The Oriental poppy is a great favourite. It appears in several varieties, mostly in shades of red or orange, but there is a white one. Most flower from May to June, but the dwarf Iceland poppy will go on till September. The plants are not long lived, so it may be better to grow them as annuals.

## Pelargonium

What do you want from a plant: flower, foliage, colour, perfume, longevity? You have it all here. I have tried, in vain, to find a phrase that does justice in describing the wonderful aromatic qualities of the Zonal pelargoniums (still widely but incorrectly called geraniums). It's not earthy, for that implies a certain mustiness or dampness, nor is it like the damp autumnal smell of chrysanthemums. It is not quite like the cinnamon perfume of the pinks and has none of the cloying sweetness of the lily, or the delicacy of the rose. In short, a good, no-nonsense, exclusive, down-to-earth trademark: one you can recognize without even looking. In fact, pelargoniums are widely used in gardens for the blind, for apart from the 'basic' there are special flavours like lemon, pineapple and peppermint.

Pelargoniums can also be grown as annuals or biennials, and are a traditional favourite for the window box, or potted for indoor use. They will enhance any border from May till October, preferring sun with some shade. You can take cuttings at any time and with care have them in flower all the year round indoors on a rota basis. Although red may be a traditional colour, they do produce a wide range, including white, pink and blue. The Zonals have a dark maroon ring on the leaf; the Regals probably produce the better flowers. The trailing ivy-leaf varieties are particularly effective in hanging baskets. Specialist growers will give you a wonderful selection from upwards of 250 varieties.

It is advisable to lift and store pelargoniums in the autumn. Cut them back and store them in pots for the winter. It is important not to overwater them, and also to ensure that the compost is new and fresh when starting new plants. Grey mould is a problem: remove all dying leaves immediately they are seen. Leaf curl is another trouble, which particularly affects 'Paul Crampel' and 'King of Denmark'. It is not a killer, but the leaves become spotted

The paper-thin petals look extremely delicate, and it is true that the oriental poppy (*Papaver orientalis*) does not like wind or rain, but it is well worth growing for its spectacular display of colour, and is an excellent early-summer plant for the back of the border. Although a perennial, it is better grown as an annual.

and crinkled, and plants affected will pass it on if cuttings are taken from them.

This does not mean that pelargoniums are more susceptible than other plants to diseases. Far from it, for on the whole they are among the healthiest plants anyone could wish to have. They have one further asset, in their coloured leaves. When the flowers fade or are affected by wet weather, the leaves seem to take over, and they give a marvellous variegated display.

### Phlox

These are plants that offer three-tier joy. They suppress weeds, their leaves form a dense low carpet, and the flowers provide an exuberant foam of colour. The Douglasii varieties (pink, white and mauve) are outstanding for the rock garden: very short, under 10cm (4in). The border types, mostly around 1m (3ft), come in a profusion of both variety and colour. The paniculatas are scented and will keep the garden in perfume from May till September. (See also page 21.)

*June*

## SHORT

### Geum

A brightly-coloured border plant, part of the rose family: hence the rose-like blooms. Mostly they are orange, scarlet or yellow. One variety, 'Mrs Bradshaw' (scarlet), won an award seventy years ago and is still very popular. They grow easily from seed, make excellent cut flowers, and will go on till October.

### Hosta Plantain lily

Hostas are most widely used as foliage and ground-cover plants, and very handsome they are, too. They make a magnificent display of leaf colour in shades of green or bluish-green, but they do require a good and fairly rich soil to flourish, and do not like too much sun. Compared with the grandeur of the foliage the flowers are apt to be overlooked, but they are worthy of notice. There are a dozen or more varieties. The tubular flowers, which flourish till July or possibly August, are mainly lavender or pale mauve in colour.

## Hypericum St John's wort

I bought my first hypericums as perennials several years ago and have always regarded them as such. But although some nurserymen still list them, the trend seems to be to include them among the shrubs, presumably because of their woody nature. The popular Rose of Sharon, *H. calycinum*, is, however, divided in spring like a perennial. Some varieties have variegated leaves. (See also page 116.)

## Scabiosa Scabious

This is well named the pin-cushion plant, by virtue of the little mound in the centre of the frilly, delicate-looking petals (mostly blue, though there are some pink or white). It is a sun lover and because it tends to spread quite rapidly should be divided every two or three years.

## Vinca Periwinkle

This is a great favourite, but is best kept away from the border. It is one of the finest plants I know for covering the ground quickly: *V. major*, or the great periwinkle, is a great hero (or offender) in this respect, and is ideal for covering an awkward slope or bank. The leaves are evergreen. The flowers, mostly blue, will last until September or October. There are some with red flowers, and a white.

## MEDIUM

## Achillea Yarrow

Probably the best of the yarrows is 'Coronation Gold' which, in addition to its mainly yellow flowers, has attractive greyish-green foliage. The flowers will thrive until September, last well when cut, and can also be dried and used for winter arrangements. It is one of the easiest of all plants to grow as it seems to thrive anywhere. Another good variety is 'Moonshine', for when the yellow flowers have gone the silvery foliage will remain for most of the year.

## Aconitum Monk's hood

The common name refers to the hooded shape of the flowers, usually blue. A slightly tricky plant, this. The secret of success is to give it a fairly sunny and well drained position. It is said to be poisonous if any part is eaten. Though this

is unlikely, there is some risk of intense irritation should any of the sap enter through a cut or broken skin.

## Anchusa

As notable for its foliage – coarse and hairy – as for its flowers, which are small and dainty. Mainly intense blue, these will last until August. Best grown in a sunny spot. (See also page 18.)

## Campanula Bellflower

Here is another multi-functional plant. Many of the varieties are intended for the rock garden,

Above: Hypericum (St John's wort) is widely used as a ground cover plant, though many varieties are somewhat shrubby and can grow to a reasonable height. Best known, perhaps, is *H. calycinum*, 'Rose of Sharon'. The one shown here, thriving among rocks, is *H. polyphyllum*, growing to only 15cm (6in).

Left: Campanula comes in a wide range of sizes and types. Some climb; others are very low growers. This one, *C. carpatica* 'Blue Chips', is a short-growing one that excels in a rock garden.

# Perennials

but they all represent a bonus for owners of chalk gardens, for they do well there provided the soil does not lack nourishment. Most varieties produce a spate of blue flowers until August or beyond, and their generous spikes of bloom make excellent subjects in a flower arrangement.

### Coreopsis

An old cottage garden favourite, this will provide masses of yellow flowers for cutting right through the summer into early autumn. There are several varieties, in different heights ranging to over 1m (3ft).

### Dictamnus Burning bush

An interesting plant, and one that is easy to grow. In America it is known as the gas plant. The novelty aspect is its party trick, for it exudes an inflammable oil, and on a warm evening a lighted match held near the plant will cause it to burst into flame, though oddly without causing any damage. When not 'performing' the dictamnus will please both eye and nose with nice spikes of lilac-coloured flowers and, as a bonus, pleasingly fragrant foliage. Naturally, requiring some heat for its fire-eating act, it is at its best from June till August.

Right: The true geranium (cranesbill) is the hardy perennial: its close relation, the pelargonium, is really a tender bedding plant. Free-flowering, with generally small blooms, it grows to 60cm (2ft) in height. *G. sanguineum*, shown here, is so named because its leaves were once believed to check bleeding.

Below: Gaillardia, the blanket flower, has large daisy-like flowers, mostly in yellow and red. They are fine plants for the border, bringing a bright display of dual colour, and also make good cut blooms.

### Gaillardia

Better known as a half-hardy annual, this plant will repay your attention. If it is given a dry and sunny position, with well drained soil it will stand up well in a drought. Flowers are mainly bright yellow or orange, with a darker, typically daisy pin-cushion centre. It will thrive until late summer. (See also page 29.)

### Geranium

Not to be confused with the pelargoniums mentioned earlier and which are still widely but wrongly called geraniums. The genuine geraniums, though closely related, are the somewhat smaller cranesbills. They are very tough, and many of them are excellent in an alpine bed or rock garden. Best known, probably, is 'Johnson's Blue', with bright blue flowers and attractively shaped foliage. Pink and red varieties are also available. Typically, it will bloom all through summer, probably till September.

### Lavatera Mallow

Another colourful plant, with large trumpet-like flowers, usually pink. It is a shrubby perennial (also known as the tree mallow) but tends to die back after flowering if the weather turns cold. Nevertheless, it does flower freely from June till September, and there is the additional benefit of pleasant, greyish, downy leaves. (See also page 41.)

## Lupinus Lupin

A member of the leguminosae family – and therefore it is not surprising that the lupin is used for agricultural purposes as well as decorative ones. The familiar spikes of flowers appear in a wide range of colours. The original ones were nearly all blue, but now they are obtainable in almost every colour and shading. They do not flourish in chalk, and they prefer a fairly rich soil. They also like room to breathe, so space them out well. They are generally at their best in time for Midsummer's Day and will go on for long after this, probably into early autumn. Because of their height they look well in a vase, but personally I prefer to see a group of them in the garden – a lovely sight, especially where there is a mixture of colours. (See also page 30.)

## Nepeta Catmint

Aromatic leaves, lavender-type flowers – not very spectacular on their own – but a gentle companion in the border. 'Feathery' is one description applied to them. I once acquired a garden where nepeta and some old – very old – roses were neighbours. My predecessor knew what he was doing, for the effect was charming.

## Pyrethrum

This plant comes in a variety of guises, as an annual or perennial. The annuals are very low-growing plants (some are more notable for their foliage than for the famous daisy-like flowers), but here we are concerned with the much taller perennial, which grows to about 60cm (2ft).

They make excellent cut flowers: the first flush will come in June, perhaps a little earlier, and that could be the end of their display. The secret is to cut back the flowering stems when they are over. New blooms will then appear, going right through till September or October. They like good, fairly rich, soil, for they are hungry feeders, as you can imagine from the rate at which they produce flowers. For best results divide them every two or three years.

## TALL

So far, the small and medium-sized plants have had it all their own way. From now on, however, the taller plants will be able to exercise some weight in the garden scene, and there are three wonderful ones to start the display of the 'big guns' in June.

## Aruncus Goat's beard

Magnificent creamy plumes of star-like flowers make this one of the most conspicuous and distinguished inhabitants of any border. Fern-like foliage is another pleasing aspect of this impressive plant, which does best in a dampish soil. Unfortunately, it does not last very long – the display is usually over by July.

Below: *Lavatera trimestris* makes a bushy plant with flowers like a single hollyhock.

Bottom: The perennial pyrethrum grows to 60cm (2ft) and is a very useful border plant. If the flowering stems are cut back when the blooms are over new growth should appear, giving colour from June till September or October.

The tall handsome spikes of delphiniums form a statuesque corner in any garden. They thrive in virtually any soil, but to avoid damage in bad weather they should be staked. They are at their best in early summer.

**Delphinium** Larkspur

What can one say that is new about these stalwarts? They are so well known, and so well loved, that it is difficult to pay adequate tribute to their worth. Their appearance at Chelsea Flower Show every May, slightly before they are due to bloom, is always one of the highlights of the vast display there.

In fact, there are developments, for the traditional blues are now being challenged by some red shades. Even more striking is the very recent introduction of a dwarf variety, 'Blue Flash', which stands under 1m (3ft) and does not need staking. And as I write, I have on my desk seed of a secret, new, unnamed variety said to be a dwarf blue and white. If this, too, is a success there will be a new trend in delphinium growing, but I doubt whether the majestic tall ones will ever be dethroned. We need them, to give dimension to a border – and they will go on flowering until September. (See also page 37.)

**Rheum** Rhubarb

A plant which is by no means so well known, or so widely stocked by nurserymen, as it should be, though everybody knows the cooking variety. This is the ornamental rhubarb, growing well over 2m (6ft) high given a shady spot by some water. Huge leaves, as big as elephant's ears, make this a spectacular specimen in any garden, provided the garden itself is big enough not to be overshadowed by it.

Clearly, it is not for everyone, or every garden, but with the immense popularity of garden pools nowadays this could break up the somewhat harsh lines of so many artificial ponds and provide a more natural look. The foliage is matched by a glorious deep red flower, which unfortunately is over by July. But if you have the opportunity, get one or two plants.

## July

By July the era of the newly sprung dwarf and front-edgers is over. From now on the medium and tall plants will attract most attention.

## MEDIUM

**Acanthus** Bear's breeches

This is a handsome plant with both its flowers and foliage: the leaf shape is recognizable in a lot of ancient Greek architecture. The leaves are dark green and the thick spikes of flowers usually deep purple: an impressive combination that will last till late summer. It flowers better in a sunny position.

**Althaea** Hollyhock

The hollyhock can be grown as an annual or biennial but, as any cottage garden will demonstrate, it can go on and on for years with little or no attention. And after all there is something delightful about a string of blooms clambering up a stem as tall as a man, or even taller. One oddity: there are many references in gardening encyclopaedias to the fact that the hollyhock is a perennial, but it is not listed as such in any of my catalogues. Start them from seed in the greenhouse in early spring, or outdoors in early summer, and you should get a fine display the following year. (See also page 36.)

## Aster

The backbone of thousands of floral displays in mid- to late summer. Where would the English garden be without the Michaelmas daisy? They are the real work-horses at this time of the year, for they will flourish almost anywhere. To get the best from them, however, they should be given a sunny site and the ground should have been well prepared – not too rich, but plenty to feed on. They also like a good drink.

There are so many good varieties it is very difficult to pick out any as outstanding. If well treated they should grow up to, and perhaps a little above, 1·5m (5ft), so it is advisable to stake them. They will quickly form clumps, so need dividing every second or third year.

Colours? Pink, blue, red, carmine, violet and white. They will go on until the frosts cut them down. There are also some smaller varieties, about one-third of the usual height. (See also page 24.)

## Astilbe

Noted for their feathery flowers, lasting throughout July and August. There are a few white varieties, and one or two pinks, but most are in deep red shades. Most people know them as spiraea, but the botanists say this is wrong. Gardeners nevertheless will undoubtedly go on asking for them by the traditional name until nurserymen remove them from the catalogues. Part shade and deep, fertile, damp soil are their main requirements, plus good rich soil.

## Chrysanthemum

Our thoughts in this section are for the shasta daisies or marguerites, beautiful white daisies with yellow centres, and of course all excellent for cutting. Good soil and plenty of sun will keep them happy. (See also page 26.)

## Echinops Globe thistle

It may be difficult to accept that this plant is of the same family as the shasta daisy, but that is the case. The name means 'like a hedgehog' and refers to the sharp spines or spikes surrounding this very attractive plant that is done such a

disservice by its ugly-sounding name. The flowers, small but densely packed, form the globe and are blue. They will outlast the greater part of summer, into early autumn.

## Eryngium Sea holly

There is something poetic about the apt common name, sea holly, and I am sure you will succumb, as I did long ago, to the architectural beauty of this lovely bluish plant. It looks fearfully spiky, but that proves no deterrent to the scores of colourful butterflies and moths that alight on those in my border, though they may have been attracted first by some adjacent buddleias. Well-drained soil is the main requirement. It makes an excellent indoor decoration for the winter when dried.

## Gypsophila Baby's breath

This is not, to my mind, an attractive plant in itself: the flowers, pink or white, are enveloped in a film of stem and leaf. In fact, the words fairy, star and veil appear among the names of different varieties. I feel it lacks character, but it is a graceful accompaniment to other plants and is very nearly essential as a background to cut flowers. It works hard at this, continuing in flower until October.

## Helenium

Yet another of the daisies, and good for cutting in a range that goes from yellow-copper-orange to mahogany. This is another that will see the summer out.

Above: The shasta daisy, *Chrysanthemum maximum*, flowers abundantly in the border.

Below: The spectacular globular heads of echinops, the globe thistle. A handsome plant, growing to 1m (3ft), it flowers in July and August.

The fibrous-rooted (Japanese) anemones tend to form clumps, so need dividing at intervals. These are mainly in pastel shades of pink or white.

### Rudbeckia

A plant that is best known as an annual or biennial, but there are some perennial versions. They grow up to 2m (6ft) or more. Striking deep gold flowers make an especially cheering sight as summer gives way to autumn. (See also page 33.)

### Yucca

A grossly underrated plant. There is a wide and dreadfully mistaken belief that its glorious white lily-like blooms appear only once in seven years. This could be because for many years thousands of them were stuck in the middle of tiny front gardens in suburban streets and never given any thought. It is more properly regarded as a shrub, though it does duty as a perennial. It has architectural value and can be a fine centrepiece. The leaves are sword-like, rather like gladiolus leaves. But it does need fairly good and well-drained soil, and it thrives in sunshine. Then it may easily bloom every year, and the flower spikes alone will come up to head height. The plants need no attention other than removing the faded flower spikes.

## *August*

### SHORT

### Anemones

The Japanese types of anemone come to the fore here, heralding the brigade of plants that will soldier on through winter. Though anemones are normally regarded as bulbs, these have roots that feel their way underground to spread the clump. Not so hardy as the better known bulbous types, they fade away in October, but they make a pretty sight while they are with us. (See also page 51 and page 60.)

### Dianthus Carnations

The border types are often grown as biennials but can be used as perennials. Planted out in autumn they will produce their wonderful clove-scented flowers in August, perhaps a little earlier, and will go on until September, or a little later, depending on conditions. There are several varieties, and all can be grown from seed. (See also page 19 and page 77.)

### MEDIUM

### *Artemisia* Wormwood

Few plants have such an array of common names: old man, lad's love, mugwort and southernwood are a few that come to mind, apart from wormwood. Its main asset is the delicious fragrance of the mainly grey and silver foliage. However, it needs not only good drainage but also dry weather and, for preference, plenty of sun to be at its best. The flowers, small and white, are really a minor detail: it is the leaf colour and perfume that

matter. Put them near some of the highly-coloured border plants, or under roses if you like, and they form a magnificent colour contrast.

## Ornamental Grasses

There is one further sector of the perennials that should be mentioned. Ornamental grasses play a large part in setting the stage of a well-planned garden, and there is a rapidly increasing interest in their scope and value. Pampas grass is undoubtedly the best known, with its graceful ostrich-feathery white plumes. Bear in mind that though most of them lose their attractive 'plumes' in winter, in many cases they do retain some semblance of a plant.

Among the better ones is *Avena candida*, with bluish-evergreen leaves. And a pleasant flower spray adds decoration for most of the summer. *Carex morrowii* has yellow-edged leaves, which retain their colour all through the year.

*Hakonchloa macra albo aurea* is a beauty with yellow and cream striped leaves having a graceful arched or hanging effect, but it is slow to get established. A quick-growing one is *Miscanthus sacchariflorus*, with leafy canes not unlike bamboo. Though it dies down, it can grow as much as 3m (10ft) in a season.

There are many more, and it is best to consult a specialist's list before deciding, but you could do worse than rely on the old favourite, bamboo, a shrubby grass that will easily and quickly form a screen or clump 3m (10ft) or more high. Or, depending on the variety you choose, you can have one growing to only 45 cm (1½ft). The leaves make a very pleasant sound when caught by the breeze and the ripe canes are ideal pea and bean sticks. But bamboo is very incursive, and quite difficult to keep under control once allowed to become overgrown – you get some idea of what it must be like in the jungle!

Ornamental grasses come in many colours and shapes, all elegant and graceful. As well as being decorative in the garden, many kinds can be cut before the seed heads ripen and preserved for use in dried flower arrangements.

# 4 *Shrubs and Trees*

## Your garden in outline

Shrubs and trees are, in effect, the permanent residents in the garden, always there, quietly watching the passing and ever-changing parade of the herbaceous plants that come and go in a year or so. There is nothing about many of them that can be regarded as spectacular – unless you choose to ignore the effect that a huge bank of rhododendrons and azaleas can have in late spring, with their combined force of eye-popping colour and intoxicating perfume.

For purposes of introduction the two groups have to be brought together and their differences explained. To the uninitiated a shrub may appear to be simply a tree that hasn't grown up. Everybody knows what a tree looks like, but how do you recognize a shrub? In fact, the difference is very simple. A tree's branches always spring from the one trunk, and some distance from the ground. A shrub does not have one centre trunk – not in this sense, anyway. The branches are formed much nearer ground level, in some cases below it, so that they emerge almost as though they were separate entities. Size has nothing to do with it: some shrubs are bigger than some trees.

Taking trees and shrubs together, there is one major difference between them and the bulbs, perennials and annuals. The herbaceous types can be removed from place to place at fairly frequent intervals, and indeed sometimes should be for their own benefit. A tree or shrub, once planted, is there for life, and it can be a very long life. Only in very rare circumstances indeed are they moved, and then it is a major operation.

There are two types of shrubs and trees: deciduous and evergreen. The deciduous ones lose their leaves in winter and form new leaf buds, followed by that delightful pale green sheen that lets us know spring is on the way. The evergreens do not keep their leaves permanently: they remain in place through the worst of the winter, as though staying on duty to

provide us with some leaf colour in the darkest days. Then, as a rule, they moult quietly in spring when there is so much activity going on among the bright young herbaceous plants that nobody notices what is happening elsewhere.

Trees and shrubs can form, so often, the focal point of your garden, irrespective of what else grows there. Be careful only to ensure that you are not overpowered by them.

One of my earlier gardening adventures was in a London suburb. The back gardens were quite small, and in the one that backed on to mine was a huge plane tree. It had thrived over the years, as plane trees do in London, and by the time I moved in had spread its wings and was casting its shade over half a dozen gardens, which probably accounted for the fact that none of us could grow very much. In some ways we

Above: One of the best of the many beautiful varieties of hydrangea is *H. villosa*, usually pale purple and normally seen at its best in August, with rather unusual flat-topped clusters of flowers.

Opposite: Rhododendrons and azaleas, underplanted with hardy geraniums and hemerocallis, make a brave spring show.

all welcomed it: in summer particularly it made a change for all of us from looking into the backs of the opposite row of houses. It was a calling post for birds from the nearby parks, and it was a focal point for all of us, though I could have wished for something more ornamental.

The point is that whoever had planted that tree, thirty or forty years previously, obviously had given no thought as to how big it would grow and what its ultimate effect would be, not only in his own garden but in the surrounding ones. It really did dominate, and of course it shut out a lot of light.

So one thing to bear in mind if you contemplate buying a tree or shrub is to make sure that it will not take over from you. One of the dangers is that the roots will not only throw up little woody mounds and make lawn-mowing difficult beneath the tree, but may also ruin a wall dividing your garden from the one next door, or even undermine the foundations of your own house.

You can, of course, have a large tree, or several of them, if your garden is big enough. From the London back yard I have mentioned we went straight to a huge four-acre garden in Kent where, a century or so earlier, someone had planted a lime tree about thirty-three metres from the house. By the time we arrived on the scene it was a vast tree, twenty metres high, perhaps more, and its gnarled old roots,

raising themselves inches out of the soil, made walking round the tree a hazardous occupation unless you looked very carefully where you were going.

But it was the ideal setting. The house and the tree were in perfect proportion to each other, and all we could do was to express our admiration for the man who had planted it. Being set at an angle from the corner of the house it did not dominate the view from the window, though we could see it. The late afternoon sun caused it to throw a shadow across the lawn, which was very pleasant, inviting us on a hot day to have our tea in a cool shady spot.

These two extremes from my own experience are, I know, rare, but they illustrate the point I am trying to make: that you should spend more time and thought on planning what to do about your trees and shrubs, and where to put them, than on any other part of the garden.

## Soil

First you must decide which shrubs are suitable for the soil conditions in your garden. For, big and strong and sturdy and tough as they are, in their own way they are just as susceptible to the chemical content of their soil as anything else that grows in it. Rhododendrons, for instance, dislike lime and are at their best on acid soil – the miles and miles of common ponticums you see along the peat-bordered roads of western Scotland tell their own story. Clematis, on the other hand, are reputed to be at their best where there is a fairly strong lime content. Almost everywhere you will be recommended to bury their roots in a small pile of builders' rubble, but some authorities disagree completely.

Here we come up against the old question of which expert to believe. It is universally accepted that heathers are acid-loving plants, and one expert of my acquaintance says quite flatly that they will die in a chalky soil. But several highly respectable specialist nurseries will offer you heathers that are tolerant of lime. And for one more example, I have one list that mentions only three viburnums, including *V. plicatum tomentosum*, that are especially useful on lime, and another declaring unequivocally that all viburnums will tolerate lime, with the single exception of *V. p. tomentosum*. So what are you to do when the experts disagree?

The natural reaction, and certainly the best plan, is to look around your immediate neighbourhood and try to find out exactly

*Acer palmatum*, the Japanese maple, is probably the best known of this large family of trees and shrubs. This one is adaptable in either category, and makes an excellent subject in a large pot or tub.

which variety it is of any plant, tree or shrub that is doing well and takes your fancy. The owner will never refuse to tell you, if he knows: gardeners who are proud of their plants are always willing to tell you everything they can about them. This method does have the drawback that you will be growing only the same things as everybody else although yours may be a better-balanced selection, but if you have got your basics right you can afford to be a little venturesome and experiment with something different. Every garden has somewhere in it a pocket of soil slightly different in content

and composition from the rest. The difference may not be significant, but it could be the key to your being successful with an 'impossible' plant.

If you are seriously planning a garden that is to be an individual one and not just run-of-the-mill, I would suggest that you carry out some soil tests, so that you can get a pretty accurate idea of what will thrive where, no matter what the neighbours grow. Until a few years ago soil testing was a very complicated business and you had to send away samples of your soil for analysis. Nowadays, however, every amateur

Specimen trees and shrubs planted between island beds of foliage plants show how interesting in colour and shape a garden without flowers can be.

can buy a kit that will give results that are accurate enough for the purpose.

## Selection and Planting

So we have decided that your trees and shrubs and the soil in which you plant them must be compatible, and that your chosen plants must be prominent in the landscape without dominating it. Your next step must be very carefully considered, for what you decide can affect the appearance of your garden for the next twenty years, perhaps more. Your choice is embarrassingly wide. You may like to have a willow, or an oak, or an elm, or a lovely *Ginkgo biloba* as a focal point at the end of the lawn. Your plan must depend entirely on the size of your garden.

Above: *Berberis darwinii* is a dual-purpose shrub, notable both for its grand display of fiery small flowers in spring and its attractive blue fruits in autumn.

Information chart 4 TREES

| NAME | HEIGHT m | HEIGHT ft | SITUATION | SOIL | CHARACTERISTICS |
|---|---|---|---|---|---|
| Acer (Maple) | 3–30 | 10–100 | sun, some shade | any, well-drained | noted for autumn foliage colouring |
| Ailanthus (Tree of Heaven) | 8 | 27 | sheltered | light, rich | fast growing; 1m (3ft)-long leaves; berries |
| Alnus (Alder) | 6 | 20 | moist | A. cordata thrives on chalk | springtime catkins; fast grower |
| Amelanchier (June berry) | 4 | 13½ | moist | lime free | A. canadensis has white springtime flowers; winter bark colour |
| *Aralia chinensis* | 2 | 7 | part shade | rich, well-drained | white flowers in autumn |
| *Araucaria araucana* (Monkey puzzle tree) | 15–25 | 50–83½ | moist | loamy | evergreen conifer |
| *Arbutus unedo* (Strawberry tree) | 2½ | 8½ | some sun | thrives on chalk | evergreen; autumn fruits |
| Betula (Birch) | 9 | 30 | part shelter | all except chalk | silver bark |
| *Carpinus betulus* (Common hornbeam) | 15–20 | 50–67 | any | clay or chalk | long-lasting leaves; can train as hedge |
| Catalpa (Indian bean tree) | 5 | 17 | sheltered | fairly good | white flowers in late summer |
| Chamaecyparis | 15 | 50 | sun | moist, well-drained | evergreen; attractive foliage; *C. lawsoniana* excellent for hedge or screen |
| Crataegus (Thorn) | 5 | 17 | any | any | can be used as hedge; very hardy |
| *Crataegus monogyna* (Hawthorn) | 5 | 17 | any | any | perfumed flowers |
| Eucalyptus (Gum tree) | 5 | 17 | sun, shelter | light | very quick grower |
| Fagus (Beech)  up to | 10 | 33½ | dry | most, especially chalk | magnificent as specimen tree or hedge |
| *Ginkgo biloba* (Maidenhair tree) | 6 | 20 | any | well-drained | fan-shaped leaves |
| Ilex (Holly) | 4 | 13½ | sun, some shade | medium, well-drained | evergreen; winter berries |
| Juniperus (Juniper) | 3 | 10 | sun | good on chalk | evergreen |
| Laburnum | 4 | 13½ | sun | light | yellow flowers in spring |
| Larix (Larch) | 6 | 20 | open | all except chalk | bright green tints in spring; autumn needles |
| Malus (Flowering crab) | 3½ | 12 | sun | any | spring flowers; autumn apples |
| Populus (Poplar) | 8 | 27 | cold, exposed | damp | tall growing; good for seaside gardens |
| Prunus | 6 | 20 | sunny | well-drained | spring flowers |
| Quercus (Oak) | 9 | 30 | any | well-drained | Q. cerris sheds leaves in summer |
| *Robinia pseudoacacia* (Common acacia) | 6 | 10 | sun | dry sandy | fragrant white flowers in June |
| Salix (Willow) | 3½ | 12 | damp | fairly heavy | Purple osier best for smaller gardens |
| Sorbus | 3–7 | 10–23½ | sun | acid or chalk | red berries in early autumn |
| Thuya | 1–4 | 3½–13½ | sun | good loam | evergreen; aromatic; hedge or specimen |
| Tilia (Lime) | 15 | 50 | sun | loamy, moist | fragrant blossom in June |

Your domain may be so small that a couple of apple trees on the lawn is as far as you can go (and don't forget that of all the items in this book, *Shrubs and Trees* is the only section that can accommodate fruit as part of its brief). An apple, pear or plum tree in the middle of the lawn, or somewhere near the end of it, will provide you with both wonderful blossom in spring and harvestable fruit at the end of summer, if not before, so don't dismiss this idea out of hand.

Or you may prefer to have a purely decorative scheme. And immediately you have the choice from a myriad of (mainly) shrubs that will provide you with colour and possibly perfume at the appropriate season, and for the rest of the year will make what might be termed an architectural feature of your garden.

With many new housing estates, it must be agreed that planting even a single tree is not a feasible proposition. But there will still be room for a few shrubs – roses are shrubs and there cannot be many gardens in Britain that have none. Nor need the owner of one of the new-style compact estate gardens limit himself to roses. The range is wide, but selection is a much more serious operation than, say, sending off an order for seeds or bulbs. They will provide you with a fleeting rainbow of colour, but your woody trees and shrubs are permanent, and the garden must to a very large extent be built around them. If you are starting a new garden from scratch, it is a good idea to plan first where you will have these cornerposts.

One factor to consider is that they will all be slow to get into their stride. True, nowadays, you can buy container-grown plants that are three or four years old and transplant them to give the effect of a mature garden overnight, but this is expensive, and there are still thousands of people who prefer to begin with young plants and watch them develop.

If you adopt this more conventional approach you must be prepared for a wait of a few years before they have matured. Because of their ultimate spread, they have to be planted several metres apart, and this means a lot of empty space for the first couple of years or so. This area is not wasted: you can effect a temporary fill-in with flowers or bulbs, or quick ground-cover plants. Indeed many of these can remain in position even when your shrubbery is worth showing off to visitors.

Trees and shrubs, once planted, will generally withstand all but the most outrageous weather conditions, but while still out of the ground they do need some care. If one arrives with the roots still shrouded in the ball of soil in which it was grown, keep this intact so far as possible: that piece of soil is its 'home' and it may not take kindly to a sudden change of environment. If there is no soil attached, you have as compensation the opportunity to inspect the roots closely. There should be a good long tap root and plenty of smaller, very fibrous ones: these are the 'feelers' that will seek out nourishment and create good root development, the secret of healthy growth. Skeletal, almost hairless root development is ominous – reject any such plant.

If the weather is frosty, try to keep your new plants in a cool (but not freezing) place under cover until you can deal with them: being dormant they will not normally come to much harm for a few days. Otherwise, if you cannot plant them straight away, heel them in. Dig a shallow trench, lay them in at an angle of approximately 45 degrees, and firm the soil back again, covering the roots. When you are ready to plant, soak the roots in a bucket of water for twenty-four hours beforehand. Never plant them dry: dried-out roots take a very long time indeed to acclimatize themselves and begin working.

With the reservation that it is unwise to plant in waterlogged soil, ensure that the surrounding soil is well moistened as soon as you have finished planting, and if the plant needs staking put the stake in first, so that you do not unwittingly drive it through the roots.

*Hydrangea macrophylla* is known as the common hydrangea, but it takes two forms, and there are many varieties. One form is the more familiar hortensia, or mop-head; the other is the flatter-shaped lace cap. This one is *H. m.* 'Générale Vicomtesse de Vibraye'.

| NAME | HEIGHT | | SITUATION | SOIL | CHARACTERISTICS |
|------|--------|-----|-----------|------|-----------------|
| | m | ft | | | |
| Aucuba | $1\frac{1}{2}$ | 5 | shade | any | evergreen foliage ; good in towns |
| Azalea | $1\frac{1}{2}$–2 | 5–7 | semi-shade | acid | spring flowering ; many are perfumed |
| Berberis (Barberry) | 1–2 | $3\frac{1}{2}$–7 | sun, part shade | any | some evergreen ; thorny ; deciduous kinds berried ; good for hedging |
| Berberis stenophylla | 2 | 7 | prefers shade | any | evergreen ; orange flowers ; thick growth |
| Buddleia (Butterfly bush) | $2\frac{1}{2}$ | $8\frac{1}{2}$ | sun | poor | fast-growing ; long flower spikes |
| Buddleia davidii | 3 | 10 | sun | poor | 'Royal Red' has profuse purple flowers |
| Calluna (Ling) | $\frac{1}{2}$ | 2 | sun | all except chalk | mostly white heather-type flowers, late summer |
| Camellia | 3 | 10 | north wall | lime-free | evergreen ; spring-flowering |
| Camellia japonica | 3 | 10 | north wall | lime-free | mainly red blooms |
| Ceanothus (Californian lilac) | 3 | 10 | sun | well-drained | mostly evergreen ; long-lasting blue flowers |
| Ceanothus 'Gloire de Versailles' | 2 | 7 | sun | well-drained | spectacular blooms |
| Chaenomeles | 2 | 7 | sun, part shade | moist | mainly pink flowers ; quince fruits |
| Chamaecyparis m. aurea | $\frac{1}{2}$ | 2 | sun | dry | evergreen ; gold foliage ; slow-growing |
| Cistus (Evergreen rock rose) | 1 | $3\frac{1}{2}$ | sun | dry, poor | evergreen ; midsummer-flowering |
| Clematis | 2–10 | 7–$33\frac{1}{2}$ | sun (shade roots) | chalk, well-drained | magnificent climbers ; wide colour range ; some bloom twice |
| Clematis montana | 10 | $33\frac{1}{2}$ | sun (shade roots) | chalk, well-drained | very vigorous ; free- and large-flowering April-June |
| Conifer vars. | 1–10+ | $3\frac{1}{2}$–$33\frac{1}{2}$+ | sun | various | mostly evergreens ; blue, green or gold foliage |
| Cornus (Dogwood) | 2 | 7 | sun, part shade | damp | notable for winter bark colour (red) ; C. alba bears white summer flowers |
| Cornus mas (Cornelian cherry) | 4 | $13\frac{1}{2}$ | sun | damp | yellow spring flowers ; autumn leaf and bark colour |
| Cotoneaster | 1–4 | $3\frac{1}{2}$–$13\frac{1}{2}$ | part shade | heavy | mostly evergreen ; autumn berries |
| Cotoneaster dammeri | $\frac{1}{2}$ | 2 | part shade | any | evergreen ; spring flowers, autumn berries ; good for ground cover |
| Cotoneaster horizontalis | 1 | $3\frac{1}{2}$ | part shade (north wall) | any | spring flowers ; autumn berries |
| Cupressocyparis leylandii (Cypress) | 1–10 | $3\frac{1}{2}$–$33\frac{1}{2}$ | sun | well-drained | evergreen ; fastest-growing conifer ; good as hedge |
| Cytisus (Broom) | $\frac{1}{2}$–3 | 2–10 | sun | all except chalk | yellow springtime bloom |
| Daphne mezereum | $1\frac{1}{2}$ | 5 | sun, shelter | light loam | scented mauve flowers in early spring ; berries later |
| Deutzia | 1–2 | $3\frac{1}{2}$–7 | sun | well-drained | prolific midsummer flowering |
| Elaeagnus p. maculata | 2 | 7 | sun, part shade | well-drained | evergreen ; golden leaves |
| Erica (Cape heather) | $\frac{1}{4}$–$\frac{1}{2}$ | 1–2 | sun | mostly acid ; some lime-tolerant | late summer flowers ; good for ground cover |
| Escallonia | 2 | 7 | sun, shelter | well-drained | mostly evergreen ; pink early-summer blooms |
| Euonymus (Spindle shrub) | 2 | 7 | sun | chalk | autumn foliage and fruits |
| Euonymus e. atropurpureus | 2 | 7 | sun | chalk | purple-red foliage ; crimson fruits |
| Forsythia | $1\frac{1}{2}$ | 5 | sun | any | yellow flowers in early spring |
| Fuchsia | 1 | $3\frac{1}{2}$ | sun, part shade | moist | bell-like, pink/purple flowers |
| Garrya elliptica | 2 | 7 | sun | well-drained | evergreen ; green/pink catkins in spring |
| Hamamelis mollis (Witch hazel) | 3 | 10 | sun, part shade | moist loam | perfumed winter flowers |
| Hebe | 1 | $3\frac{1}{2}$ | sun | well-drained | evergreen ; fast-growing ; mainly pink/white flowers over long summer periods |

There is a way of getting almost instant coverage with even very young plants, and I discovered it by accident. A very knowledgeable friend who showed me round his garden was busily making notes as we went of the plants I especially admired, telling me that I must have some, or cuttings from them, for my new garden. I had forgotten the incident when one day he rang to say that my plants were ready for collection. We had no space available at the time, so hastily dug out a long narrow bed, about a metre wide, across the lawn, and bore home our new treasures.

There must have been about fifty of them, perhaps more, a mixture of all sorts, and not all just cuttings: some buddleias, dogwood, broom, daphne, euonymus, eleagnus and many more, including a number of variegated-leaved perennials. We spaced them out, staggered to give each as much room as possible, planted them, and left them to their fate while we got on with more urgent tasks around the new house.

| NAME | HEIGHT m | HEIGHT ft | SITUATION | SOIL | CHARACTERISTICS |
|---|---|---|---|---|---|
| ebe 'Blue Gem' | 1 | 3½ | sun | well-drained | blue-flowered variety ; good for hedging |
| edera (Ivy) | 3½ | 12 | part shade | poor | strong evergreen ; hardy climber |
| edera helix | 3½ | 12 | part shade | poor | variegated leaves |
| ibiscus (Tree allow) | 2 | 7 | sun | rich, well-drained | late-flowering, mainly red/blue ; good for hedges |
| ydrangea | 2 | 7 | sun | all except chalk | magnificent flower heads, mainly blue or pink |
| ypericum (St John's wort) | 1 | 3½ | sun | any | excellent ground cover |
| ypericum calycinum (Rose of Sharon) | ½ | 2 | sun | dry | evergreen ; yellow flowers, excellent ground cover |
| ex (Holly) | 3 | 10 | sun, part shade | light | evergreen ; most have winter berries |
| asminum (Jasmine) | up to 10 | 33½ | sun | any ; rich | sweet-scented climber, winter or summer |
| uniperus (Juniper) | up to 5 | 17 | some sun | good on chalk | evergreen ; attractive berries ; aromatic foliage |
| avandula (Lavender) | ½–1 | 2–3½ | sun | not too rich | sweet scent ; good for drying |
| onicera (Honeysuckle) | 4 | 13½ | part shade | moist, well-drained | mainly climbing ; sweet perfume |
| agnolia | 2 | 7 | sun, shelter | all except chalk | magnificent white blooms tinged with pink, some perfumed |
| ahonia | 1½ | 5 | sun, part shade | any | evergreen ; flowering holly-type plant |
| ahonia aquifolium (Oregon grape) | 1½ | 5 | shade | any | evergreen ; yellow flowers in spring ; grapes in autumn |
| earia (Daisy bush) | 1 | 3½ | sun, part shade | well-drained | evergreen ; daisy-like flowers in late summer ; good for hedges |
| aeonia (Paeony) | 1½ | 5 | sun | rich | yellow or pink spring flowers, attractive foliage |
| arthenocissus (Virginia creeper) | 12 | 40 | sun | any | climber ; red autumn foliage |
| hiladelphus (Mock ange) | 1½ | 5 | sun, part shade | light or chalk | sweet-scented white/cream flowers |
| eris | 2 | 7 | shade | light, lime-free | evergreen ; fragrant spring flowers |
| otentilla | 1 | 3½ | sun, part shade | any | yellow flowers May-October ; good for border |
| otentilla fruticosa | 1 | 3½ | sun, part shade | any | white flowers ; good for hedging |
| yracantha (irethorn) | 3 | 10 | sun | well-drained | climber ; spectacular berries after spring flowers |
| hododendron | 1–4 | 3½–13½ | shade | damp, acid | deciduous or evergreen ; magnificent blooms, some perfumed, spring and summer |
| hus (Sumach) | 2–3 | 7–10 | sun, part shade | sandy loam | brightly coloured foliage summer/autumn |
| ambucus (Elder) | 4 | 13½ | part shade | any | white spring flower ; summer berries ; good for wine making |
| orbus | 6 | 20 | sun | any | spring flowers, autumn berries |
| ringa vulgaris ilac) | 2–5 | 7–17 | sun | chalk | fragrant white or purple flowers in spring |
| marix (Tamarisk) | 2–3 | 7–10 | sun | light loam | graceful foliage ; small pink flowers in summer |
| xus baccata | 2–5 | 7–17 | sun | chalk | evergreen foliage, mostly golden ; good for hedging |
| ournum | 1½–2½ | 5–8½ | sun, part shade | chalk | wide range of flowers, berries, foliage |
| burnum davidii | 1 | 3½ | sun, part shade | well-drained | evergreen ; summer flowers, winter berries |
| burnum x rkwoodii | 2–3 | 7–10 | good against wall | moist loam | evergreen ; pink/white spring flowers |
| isteria | 6–9 | 20–30 | sun | good loam | blue flowers in early summer ; climber |
| isteria sinensis hinese wisteria) | 10–12 | 33½–40 | sun | good loam | lilac flower spikes May-June ; strong growth |

It was a hot dry summer and we did make one concession. We kept them well watered, and how well they repaid us for our trouble. We had very few losses indeed but the happy surprise was that they grew in towards each other and in no time at all we had a very colourful 'nursery bed' that was one of the main features of the garden. There was no plan to it. It just happened that the plants were of differing heights and colours, and the variegated leaves of many of them added to the effect. They were hopelessly overcrowded in terms of permanency, but by the following year we had prepared a special bed two or three metres wide. We transplanted some and left the remainder intact. They, with more room to breathe, immediately spread their wings, and that improvised border is still a feature of the garden, and the new shrubbery likewise has prospered.

The moral of all this is don't be afraid to plant closely so that you get some immediate effect,

Above: Mahonias are often confused with berberis, but have no prickly spines, though their leaves are not unlike the holly. *M. aquifolium* bears yellow-bronze flowers in spring and blue berries in autumn — excellent for jam-making.

# Shaping and pruning shrubs and hedges

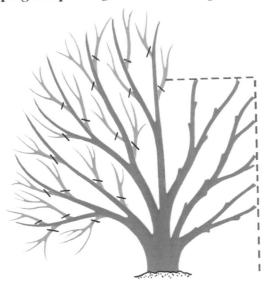

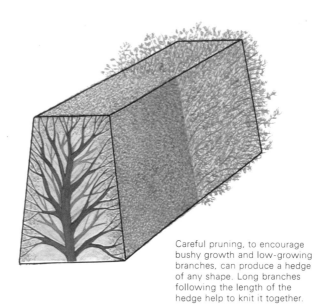

Careful pruning, to encourage bushy growth and low-growing branches, can produce a hedge of any shape. Long branches following the length of the hedge help to knit it together.

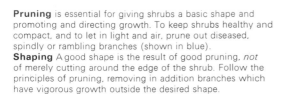

**Pruning** is essential for giving shrubs a basic shape and promoting and directing growth. To keep shrubs healthy and compact, and to let in light and air, prune out diseased, spindly or rambling branches (shown in blue).
**Shaping** A good shape is the result of good pruning, *not* of merely cutting around the edge of the shrub. Follow the principles of pruning, removing in addition branches which have vigorous growth outside the desired shape.

and be prepared to discard some of your plants after a year or so. You may not need to throw them out completely. It is surprising how many odd corners you can find in even the smallest garden for one individual plant.

Because nurserymen, for all their love of the subject, are essentially commercially minded, it is natural that more attention should be paid to quick-moving stock. I believe it was because of the greater promotion afforded bulbs and seeds that it took me such a long time to realize that there is, in practice, a wider choice of trees and shrubs than of any other kind of plant. If you live at the seaside, and your house has the full benefit of unrestricted sea views across the promenade and all that that implies, such as gallons of spray and a howling gale, will any of your seeds or bulbs survive? What will give protection to plants in the lee, and come up for more? Cotoneaster will. So will euonymus. So will escallonia, though this one would appreciate a little protection itself.

Or do you live in a town area, with impoverished soil and no means of adding the necessary humus that will make it a fitting home for your bright summer flowers? Your annuals or bedding plants will put up some kind of show, struggling against all the odds, but neither they nor you are likely to be very happy. But give a trial to *Polygonum baldschuanicum*, much more easily pronounced as Russian or mile-a-minute vine, and once it gets established it will cover everything in sight with myriads of little pinkish-white flowers, adding up to a pretty formidable sight.

Or have you a boggy area? Few plants relish wet feet, but the salix (willow) is an obvious choice in trees. And I can recommend one shrub, *Cornus alba*, the white-flowered dogwood, that will fill the gap here, and as a bonus will provide plenty of flowers for the house in summer and red foliage and/or bark as an encore in autumn. What other plants are so versatile or so busy on your behalf over such a long period?

Do you wish to make a strong natural division to mark the boundary of your property, but do not relish being shut in by a fence or wall? There can be only one answer: a hedge, and there are dozens of subjects from which to choose. Some roses make a fine hedge, likewise several varieties of berberis and cotoneaster (one of which, *C. hybrida pendula*, nominally a shrub, can also be grown as a small tree and so bring an extra dimension to your hedge to break up the line: it is an evergreen carrying hundreds of red berries in autumn and winter). And who could resist the so-called common beech, *Fagus sylvatica*? Bright green leaves in spring turn to those lovely copper shades in autumn and remain through winter – and it thrives anywhere, except on the heaviest of clays.

Perhaps you fancy something in tubs, something movable to provide a change of view, to form a contrast to the lawn, or furnish a patio? Plenty of fuchsias thrive in these conditions.

There are other bonuses, too. You can choose both trees and shrubs to give you an outline shape in half a dozen forms: spreading, round, upright, erect (less spreading than the upright ones), pyramid shape or weeping, or even prostrate, which means they are good for ground cover. You can have spring-flowering subjects – think how almond blossom brings joy to so many streets in towns and cities – and those that show leaf and bark colour, or a cascade of berries, in autumn. Those same city streets come to life in late summer with the rowan, or mountain ash, and its mass display of berries.

There are dozens that flower, and many of them are perfumed flowers, too. There are others whose foliage is scented. There are some

that specialize in certain conditions of soil or situation: chalk, clay, sand, wet, dry, sunny or shady. Some will climb a wall, although they may need support in this exercise, and others will remain doggedly close to the ground. As we have seen, some keep their leaves, and even offer flower, through the winter. They will all bring grace and dignity, and a touch of exclusiveness, to your garden.

This section has to be slightly out of balance, because there are more varieties and types of shrub for the garden than there are trees. Also, they are far more practical. A tree can easily need twenty years or more to attain a respectable size, and few of us can afford that amount of time before we can see what we regard as a worthwhile display. Shrubs, on the other hand, are generally smaller, more manageable and more adaptable, and of course they are far quicker to mature and take their full place in

Above: The sorbus is notable for its prolific display of berries. There are several varieties, and between them they produce flowers and berries from May till October. This is *Sorbus hybrida*.

Opposite: One of the best loved clematis is 'Ville de Lyon'. Its carmine colouring stands out against a wall, and it flowers from May to September.

This maple, with its scarlet autumn leaves, is one of the most eye-catching in the entire range, though it is only 1½m (5ft) high, with a similar spread. It is *Acer palmatum heptalobum* 'Osakazuki'.

your decorative scheme. Both are long-term investments. Given freedom from disaster, like Dutch elm disease or the dreaded honey fungus, they will flourish for years in the same place, saving you no end of labour in cultivating that part of the ground, and paying rent in that their fallen leaves will provide costless benefits for your soil, whether left for the worms to drag down and aerate the soil or gathered up and used as compost.

So let us go into our discussion on types for situations – and first I must warn you that some varieties of shrubs also rank as trees, and vice versa. Most cotoneasters, for instance, are undoubtedly shrubs, but one, *C. hybrida pendula*, is generally regarded as a tree, and is an excellent one, too, for a small garden. Conversely, there are some trees that can equally well be classed as shrubs. Acers provide a classic example. Some of them are definitely trees, but the Japanese maples are all classed as shrubs, though they are the same family. The crataegus is the thorn tree, but thorn hedges are obviously shrubs, and even the willow (salix) has both types in its repertoire.

## Trees

### Acer Maple

*A. campestre* is likely to be the best for your purpose. It is also known as the field or hedge maple, which explains its main uses: have it as an outsize 'dot plant' in a hedge, and you will get yellow or red foliage in autumn. Fairly small – about 6m (20ft). *A. platanoides*, the Norway maple, has yellow flowers in spring and yellow or red autumn foliage. It is higher than *A. campestre* and rapidly grows to about 10m (35ft). *A. hersii* is famous for its marbled-effect bark as well as its autumn colour. Quite a small tree – maximum 6m (20ft). But probably the maple best known as a name is *A. palmatum*, a half-breed for our purposes as it can be either a tree or a shrub. It is the famous Japanese maple, and there are many varieties of it. Most of them are a convenient size, roughly 2m (6ft), and if you have room get three or four of them and ensure yourself a wonderful and slightly varied display of foliage 'fireworks' to round off the late summer and autumn.

### Ailanthus Tree of Heaven

A well known but seldom recognized tree. It

grows fast to about 8m (25ft), tolerates a polluted atmosphere, and has very large leaves almost a metre long. Some bear red berries.

### Alnus Alder
*A. glutinosa* is the common type of alder growing to about 6m (20ft). The alders do well in moist conditions. *A. cordata* is also very useful on chalk.

### Amelanchier June berry
Like the alder, this one thrives in moist conditions. It can also be obtained in shrub form. *A. canadensis* has a mass of white flowers in spring and when the leaves have gone reddish-coloured branches relieve the winter drabness. About 3–4m (10–12ft).

### Aralia chinensis
A dwarf tree that is much shorter than a good many shrubs, growing to barely 2m (6ft). An attraction is the stalks of white flowers in early autumn, from August to October.

### Arbutus Strawberry tree
This one is a real beauty. *A. unedo* is the best for most purposes. With a maximum height of about 2·5m (8ft), it is another that is often referred to as a shrub. Not much of a display in summer, but it produces both leaves and strawberry-like fruits in autumn, even as late as November. A further bonus is that it is evergreen.

### Betula Birch
Everybody knows this one. The 'silver' and 'paper' ones are perhaps the most popular. *B. pendula*, with graceful hanging branches and white bark, is a little tall for most gardens at 9m (30ft). *B. papyrifera*, very similar in appearance, is a metre or more on top of that. There is, however, one that is ideal for a small area and looks wonderful on a lawn: *B. pendula youngii*, a short, weeping, dome-shaped birch whose branches reach to the ground. This will grow to about 5m (16ft).

### Carpinus Common hornbeam
*C. betulus* is rather tall growing for most family gardens, but if caught and trimmed in time makes a good hedge, similar to the beeches, as the leaves last well into winter. Some varieties are useful as specimen trees, notably *C. columnaris* and *C. pyramidalis* – the descriptions speak for themselves – each about 6m (20ft).

### Catalpa Indian bean tree
This one spreads to at least its own height and is very spectacular in late summer with a display of white flowers, rather like foxgloves, but these do not normally appear until the tree is well established. It grows to about 5m (16ft) and can go higher in rich soil.

### Crataegus Thorn
Can be either tree or shrub, and is beautiful as either. *C. monogyna* is known to everyone as the hawthorn, the quickthorn, or the may. Leave it as a tree and it provides a wonderful feast for eye and nose in late spring and early summer with perfumed white flowers; in autumn it produces colourful berries. It grows to about 7m (23ft). Prune hard back soon after planting to give a good bottom as a hedge and you will have no need to worry about marauding dogs and cats!

### Eucalyptus Gum tree
This is one of my favourites, not particularly for its perfume but because of the way it gets down

Most garden plants earn their place because of their attractive flowers or foliage. But with some even the bark is beautiful, and few shrubs or trees can beat the birch, *Betula pendula*, for its all-round beauty: graceful leaves, and contrasting colours in the bark.

to work very quickly. Thick, glossy, blue-green leaves shoot up very rapidly: a friend who bought some was astonished to find they grew about 1m (3ft) in a year. They are so eager that they really need restraining, so it is advisable to prune them back in the first couple of years to give them a chance to branch and make a sturdy base. There are several varieties, all evergreen. *E. gunnii*, the best known, can reach 5m (16ft) and is very hardy. *E. citriodora* has a refreshing lemony perfume but needs protection as it is rather tender.

### Fagus Beech
*F. sylvatica*, the so-called common beech, and perhaps the best loved, is the one with the wonderful copper autumn foliage and bright green springtime leaves. As a specimen tree it will easily reach 5–6m (16–20ft), but if well pruned in the early stages forms the familiar picturesque hedge.

### Fraxinus Ash
You may not want an ash because most of them do grow to rather a great height for ordinary gardens, but there are so many varieties, and they are so widely known, that they virtually force their way into this list. *F. excelsior*, the common ash, can grow up to about 9m (30ft) though there is a weeping version only about half this height. The flowering ash, *F. mariesii*, is also quite small and carries a fine display of white flowers around Midsummer's Day.

### Laburnum
The laburnum has a distinction in that it is one of the few trees whose botanical name is also the common one. In fact, I wonder how many people know it by its other name of golden rain. Those lovely drops of yellow flowers in early summer make it one of our most popular small trees: I have one that is well established yet it is only about 2·5m (8ft) tall. Yet in a way the laburnum does not deserve its popularity, for it is an uncongenial plant. According to an old wives' tale it is poisonous to everything within its reach, and there is a germ of truth in this. Certainly, neither the owner nor his child or pet must eat any of it – and if you notice, few other plants grow beneath it.

### Malus Flowering crab
Malus justifies a place in every garden, no matter how small. The spring flowers are a tonic and in the autumn their brightly coloured fruits are a temptation to small boys – until they have

Right: Mature trees and shrubs are not only lovely to look at – in the heat of summer they protect shade-loving plants and provide a cool, restful spot in the garden.

Malus, the crab apple, produces dainty springtime flowers and colourful small apples in late summer — most of them inedible raw but useful in preserves. 'John Downie' is probably the best variety; certainly it is one of the most colourful and prolific.

eaten one raw. Nevertheless, they are edible: crab apple jelly is a famous home-made delicacy. 'Golden Hornet' and 'John Downie' are best for this purpose. Top height is about 3·5m (12ft).

## Platanus London plane
This is one of the maple family, but without the leaf colour we generally associate with them. Very hardy, it can easily reach over 9m (30ft).

## Populus Poplar
Mostly we see poplars in country districts, their leafy erect branches acting as elevated windbreaks while leaving ample space below. But

here, too, the tree can become a shrub with training, and poplar hedges, though quite rare, do exist. *P. alba* is a good one for this, for it can be pruned back heavily. Very useful for seaside gardens, as it is tolerant to chalk and resistant to spray.

## Prunus
The partner to the malus family – the flowering plums, cherries and almonds. Growing conditions are much the same, and there are so many to choose from I can only say the imagination boggles. Go to a nursery or garden centre, pick out those that appeal most to you, and carry them home in triumph and expect-

ation. Most flower in spring, but *P. subhirtella autumnalis* is the autumn cherry, which blooms on most days through winter, offering sprays for cutting. Height – about 6m (20ft).

## Quercus Oak

An oak arouses feelings of pride and patriotism in much the same way that the rose does, but on a grander scale. And an oak is not impossible, even in a modest garden. Some are reckoned to grow no more than about 3.5m (12ft) at most. One, *Q. coccifera*, ranks as a shrub, grows slowly to only about 2m (6ft) and is evergreen. I have never had one, but I am told it is superb near a rock garden.

One I do know, almost too well, is *Q. cerris*, the turkey oak, for I inherited one as near neighbour to a lawn and flower beds. It is reputed to be the fastest growing of the oaks, and it was already well above 6m (20ft) when I first made its acquaintance. It cast a nice shade, without being overpowering, for the lowest branches were quite high up, but one point we had never read in books is that it sheds its leaves at the most awkward time – in midsummer. They are tough leaves, too, and made the lawn and beds look dreadfully untidy until we swept them up.

## Robinia pseudoacacia Common acacia

The 'genuine' acacia is the shrub most of us know as the wattle, which sometimes takes tree form. Fragrant white flowers in June are an irresistible magnet to bees; it is also known as the locust tree.

## Salix Willow

Another dual-purpose subject, for some varieties are trees and others shrubs. An obvious choice for a damp site, or beside a stream or pond. You may not want the best known, *S. alba caerulea*, for this is the one from which cricket bats are made, and it grows to over 9m (30ft). *S. a. tristis* – the golden weeping willow – is a magnificent one, but again rather large and about the same height. One that will hit you for six is *S. a. purpurea pendula*, a mouthful that describes the purple osier: purple bark, blue-green leaves, weeping habit, and only about 3.5m (12ft) to the top of its dome shape.

## Sorbus

The most familiar member of this family is *S. aucuparia*, the mountain ash or rowan. It has attractive foliage and hosts of bright red berries in late summer/early autumn – a magnet to birds, which devour them as soon as the weather closes in. It is particularly good in acid soil but succeeds almost anywhere, reaching 5m (16ft) in good conditions. Another popular type is *S. aria*, the whitebeam, which is a champion for chalk. A feature is the changing colour of the leaves: grey, green and gold. Again there is an abundance of berries, darker than the mountain ash. It grows to about the same height.

## Tilia Lime

I do not know the varietal name of my old lime. If I invent one, it shall be *T. poeticus*, for it was a poem. Those lovely long yellow lines of June blossom emitted a wonderful soft perfume, especially in the morning sun. The leaves sang softly in the breeze, and for weeks on end there was the background hum of the bees busily working the blossom.

On a more mundane note, limes tend to drip a sticky substance like aphid honeydew. There was a row of limes flanking our road, and many

This mass of white blossom comes from one of the smaller flowering cherries, *Prunus* 'Shimidsu Sakura', which grows to 4½m (15ft) and flowers in May.

107

which has orange flowers. They will grow to about 2m (6ft).

### Buddleia Butterfly bush
This one grows very fast and produces wonderful flower spikes in the course of a season. For best results prune hard back in spring: at first you won't believe it can recover so quickly! *B. davidii* is one of the best known species: 'Royal Red' one of its finest forms. They all grow above head height and are a wonderful stand-by as they prosper in poor soil.

### Calluna
One of the heathers, this is excellent for ground cover, and naturally dislikes lime. Most of them bear white flowers in late summer. 'H. E. Beale' has soft pink double flowers on long spikes, excellent for cutting.

### Camellia
Camellias are acid-soil subjects, usually flowering from March onwards. They are evergreen, and some will grow to about 3m (10ft). Most are hardy. The *C. japonicas*, or common camellias, are widely grown and one of the best is *C.* 'Adolphe Audusson', with glorious blood-red blooms. *C.* 'Apollo', red and white, is another excellent variety. Most camellias are in shades of red, but 'Royal White' is perhaps the best white. Camellias are especially useful against a north wall, where they are protected from the surprisingly dangerous spring morning sun.

### Ceanothus Californian lilac
Perhaps it is fortunate that this is intended to be largely a personal chronicle, for I need make no

Top: *Buddleia davidii* is known as the butterfly bush because of the attraction its close spikes of bloom have for these insects. It grows rapidly after hard pruning and thrives anywhere, even on poor or chalky soil.

Above: There are many forms of camellia. One of the best, particularly for growing on a patio, is *C. japonica* 'Adolphe Audusson', whose deep rose blooms show up vividly against a stone background.

accidents were caused by vehicles skidding on it as they rounded a sharp bend. One variety, *T. euchlora*, is free from this defect. It grows to about 9m (30ft). You can appreciate why autumn should be called the fall when you see an old lime shedding its leaves. Collect them quickly: you will help your compost along enormously. One widely recommended is *T. petiolaris*, the weeping silver lime, which is sufficient description.

## Shrubs

The remainder of this section is devoted to shrubs and their various uses, of which there are plenty. Some shrubs give you double value as they are useful in more than one category: quick-reference lists in this chapter are a guide to these uses.

### Aucuba
A hardy evergreen foliage shrub; will grow almost anywhere, in dense shade and any soil, and if planted in numbers will make a close-knit plantation.

### Azalea
See *Rhododendron*.

### Berberis Barberry
Barberries are rather thorny, good for hedging and will grow anywhere that is not too damp. Some are evergreen, notably *B. stenophylla*,

Left and above: The pale blue *Ceanothus thyrsiflorus* is very hardy, and its myriads of flowers are a magnet to bees.

secret of my regard for this shrub. Wonderful blue flowers will last all summer until the frosts. Some are a deep blue – *C. burkwoodii* is one – but most are of a paler colour. Bees love them: two friends were talking (or trying to) near a shrub and one turned to me and asked, quite seriously, 'Can't you stop those bees? We can't hear ourselves speak!' 'Gloire de Versailles' produces perhaps the most spectacular show of flowers, but there is little to choose between any of them. This one is deciduous; most are evergreen. *C. Cascade* is well named for its long flower stem, bright blue. In some districts this is evergreen in a mild winter. *C. thyrsiflorus*, also bright blue, believed to be the oldest in cultivation, is a very hardy one. They prefer a south wall and will grow in any well drained soil.

### Chaenomeles
Known by a wealth of other names – cydonia, japonica and quince – this is one of the finest of spring-flowering shrubs. The host of varieties makes selection very difficult. 'Hearn's Pink Dawn' is one of the lesser-known ones but well worth trying to get. It is a double, but many others are single flowered. Flowers are mostly in pink or red. Some varieties produce fruits – these are delicately perfumed, and excellent for flavouring or jam-making, but not for serving on their own.

### Cistus Evergreen rock rose
Most of these grow to between 60 and 120cm (2 and 4ft). Most offer white or pink flowers around midsummer. One of the hardiest is *C. laurifolius*: white flowers with a yellow centre and dark green leaves, reaching up to 2m (6ft). I wonder if that phrase about wasting sweetness on the desert air was prophetic about *Cistus × purpureus*. This hybrid won an award a little over fifty years ago, but it has been with us for nearly 200 years! If you are curious as to the reason for the delay, get one, watch its crimson and chocolate flowers (admittedly, not a very attractive sounding combination) unfurl and then make your decision. You will probably be as puzzled as I am!

### Clematis
There are so many varieties that it is really impossible to give more than a scant appraisal. They appear in nearly every colour, even yellow (*C. orientalis*). Chief among the whites are *C. henryi*, 'Miss Bateman', and 'Marie Boisselot'. The blues include 'Lady Betty Balfour',

'Lasurstern', 'The President' and *C. jackmanii* (all dark), and 'Lady Northcliffe' and 'Mrs Hope' (light). Reds are headed by 'Ville de Lyon', 'Barbara Jackman' and 'Vyvyan Pennell', with 'Gipsy Queen' superb among the purples, and 'Comtesse de Bouchaud' and 'Nelly Moser' leading the pinks. Keep them well tied in, so that their heavy flower heads have some support. They like sun, but it is generally accepted that the roots need shading.

'Clematis wilt' is a mystery disease that cuts down many young plants for a year or so, and then they appear to recover. As far as I am aware there is no known reason, and no real preventative, but I wonder if conditions have something to do with it. In one garden I was forever plagued with it, but in my present one I have so far gone three years without trouble. I have followed an old dodge by giving them plenty of water, which may account for the improvement.

### Cornus mas Cornelian cherry
Comes to life in early spring with yellow flowers on its bare twigs. Being one of the dogwoods, it

Opposite: Clematis, magnificent on its own, is equally effective when trained with another plant. This picture shows the effect of intermingling the white flowers and vivid green foliage of *Viburnum opulus* 'Sterile' with the deep lavender blue of clematis 'Lasurstern'.

Below: Cistus (rock roses) are particularly useful for small gardens. Evergreen and mostly hardy, they flower in June and July. A dry situation and poor soil suits them, and if grown in pots they can be transplanted at any time. They are, in effect, ground cover plants, barely 45cm (1½ft) high. This colourful version is *Cistus × purpureus*.

Above: Cornus,
the dogwoods, are notable
for their colourful bark —
a useful quality in
winter and early spring.

Below: *Cotoneaster
horizontalis* is a popular
ground cover shrub, with
masses of autumn berries.
Only 60cm (2ft) high,
it spreads to over 10m (33ft).

will have coloured leaves and bark in autumn. The cherries are edible, if you can beat the birds to them!

### Cotoneaster

One of the most widely grown shrubs, usually as ground cover or hedges. It is tolerant of almost any condition and offers a magnificent show of berries in autumn. Most are evergreen. *C. dammeri*, very low-growing indeed, and *C. horizontalis*, about 1m (3ft) high are probably the best known. Both have white flowers in May, with red berries in autumn. *C. dammeri* is evergreen.

### Cytisus Broom

Broom is a familiar sight everywhere. It demands sun but will accept most soil conditions except extreme chalk. Take your pick from a dozen or more. They differ in size but most of them are yellow or golden in flower, chiefly in spring, though some appear in summer. *C. purpureus*, as the name suggests, is purple-flowered.

### Daphne mezereum

One of the best known spring-flowering shrubs, which has sweet-scented purplish flowers in February/March. It also produces fruits, but don't eat them – they are poisonous.

### Deutzia

An easy-to-grow shrub, flourishing almost everywhere, and mostly flowering in June, very prolifically. I think 'Mont Rose' is the best, with very deep pink flowers, bordering on purple.

### Elaeagnus

An evergreen foliage shrub, averaging about 1·5m (5ft). *E. ebbengei* has grey-green leaves; *E. pungens maculata* will retain golden leaves through the winter.

### Erica Cape heather

There are so many heathers you could probably fill an acre with one plant of each popular variety, planted closely, and still have plenty left over. And what a wonderful display you would have! We automatically think of Scotland and the peat lands, but they are not all peat-lovers. Some of the *E. carnea* varieties – on the whole the best known – are lime-tolerant. You can get them in shades of red, pink and white, all ground-hugging and flowering mostly through the winter. *E. carnea* itself generally appears in February, with a profusion of lovely deep purple flowers. The many varieties of *E. calluna* and *E. cinerea* form the bulk of the traditional acid-loving plants in an even wider range of colour, though much the same size individually. Most of them are late summer-flowering.

Not a flower in sight, yet this is one of the most colourful scenes you could hope to
find in a garden: a remarkable combination of heathers and conifers.

## Escallonia

Escallonias will make you hedges or individual bushes. They are fast-growing, and excellent for seaside gardens. An assortment of pink, red or crimson flowers is yours, according to choice of variety. Apart from the glory of their blooms, they keep their leaves through the winter. 'Apple Blossom' and 'Donard Seedling' are about the best.

## Euonymus

*E. europaeus* is the familiar spindle shrub. *E. e. atropurpureus* turns from purple to a vivid red in autumn, with crimson fruits. They thrive in chalk.

## Forsythia

This is a shrub that seems to thrive in any conditions. Its mass of little yellow flowers appearing before the leaves is always a glorious sight on an early spring day. The most prolific is probably *F. intermedia* 'Lynwood', about 1·5m (5ft) tall; the flowers are excellent for cutting.

## Fuchsia

There is – or was – a widespread belief that fuchsias are essentially plants for indoors, or at best in well-sheltered spots. That may apply to some, but most are perfectly capable of withstanding a pretty hard winter. 'Mrs Popple' is one that comes to mind as being particularly independent of shelter. Although their bell-like flowers differ slightly in shape and colour, all fuchsias have this unusual and graceful 'ballet dancer' effect. The colours range mainly from pink to deep purple. They are extremely adaptable. Most will grow indoors or out; they will fill a hanging basket, form weeping standards on a lawn or climb wherever you wish, up to about 6m (20ft). If buying, try to spend half a day at a specialist nursery. You will find them irresistible and undoubtedly will come away with more than you had intended to buy! Many of the popular modern hybrids are descended from the tender *F. fulgens*, one of the first fuchsias to be introduced. Frequently, cuttings taken in September will reach full stature within a year.

## Garrya elliptica

One of the most gracefully unusual evergreens, famous for its catkins. Given a sunny, well drained spot it will grow well over 2m (6ft). It never needs pruning, except for a little thinning, and bears a profusion of green and pink-edged catkins all through early spring.

## Hamamelis Witch hazel

This is mainly winter-flowering with clusters of fragrant yellow bloom: very prolific, very fragrant, and very unusual in the peculiar twisted form of the petals. Makes a good colourful picture amid a bed of ericas. *H. mollis* is the best known.

## Hebe

A fast-growing evergreen, known as veronica until comparatively recently. 'Blue Gem' is a good hedging plant, low-growing and showing plenty of bright blue flower. It is an excellent seaside plant, given some shelter. There are several varieties, most of them around 1m (3ft) in height, usually showing white flowers, though there are some blues and a few purple. An exception, and a very good one, is 'Great Orme', with bright pink flowers and long, tapering leaves.

## Hedera Ivy

Ivy once had an old wives' tale reputation for being damaging to the house walls to which it clings. With the proviso that it may help a crumbling one further along the road to ruin, this can now be refuted. It will grip but not

Above: *Hamamelis mollis,* the witch hazel.
Opposite: Fuchsias' flower formation differs in almost every variety; the colourings are mainly from scarlet to purple.
Below: *Hebe speciosa gauntletii.*

115

Top: The Persian ivy, *Hedera colchica*, is very vigorous and grows almost anywhere. This is *H. dentata variegata*.

Above: Hypericums are versatile plants, offering colour in spring and, in many cases, fruits in autumn.

Opposite: One of the most majestic of the many varieties of hydrangea is *H. macrophylla mariesii*; it grows to 2m (7ft).

harm its host. It is very hardy and very tough: one of my so far unfulfilled tasks has been to open up a view along the garden by removing an old ivy-covered fence, for I haven't the heart. The ivy is tough, but by no means unpleasant. It has a splendid little flower, totally insignificant until you get close to it, and I am not convinced that its removal would improve the view, so it will stay. I don't know for certain, but I suspect that my guest is *H. colchica*, with big, dark green leaves and obvious determination to live to be a hundred!

There is another common ivy, *H. c. variegata*, where the leaves are variegated, having yellow on the edge. This is good as a ground-cover plant. A further type, *H. helix*, has a gold overtone; in this category, though with a somewhat different colour scheme, comes *H. h.* Glacier, with white and grey-green leaves.

### Hibiscus Tree mallow

Well known as a perennial, but also an excellent shrub, it is known as the tree mallow to distinguish it from the herbaceous variety. The shrub version is late-flowering, from August to September. A majestic plant, whether used solo or in borders, and ideal for use in tubs. Flowers are mainly red or blue. 'Blue Bird' is perhaps the best of them. 'Red Heart' is white with a maroon centre, and 'Woodbridge' is a bold

crimson. You may also know it as the tree hollyhock. It will grow to about 2m (6ft).

### Hydrangea

This is one of those rare plants for which dead-heading is a crime. The secret of continued success is to let the old faded flower head remain on the stem as long as possible – even in its dead and dried state it does not look repulsive – the purpose of this exercise being to protect the young buds from frost, to which they are susceptible. The sacrifice of neatness is well repaid, for hydrangea blooms must rank among the most magnificent of all.

It is largely true that the colour of your flowers will depend on the type of soil in which they are growing. Broadly, you will get blue flowers on acid or peaty soil, and pink ones on lime. But there are some white ones, which presumably thrive on neutral soils and change their colour if they go slightly over the border! Most of them are the familiar globular flowers, the hortensia varieties, but there are the dainty lacecaps, with smaller flowers on a flatter surface and different colours in the centre. All flower from midsummer, some well into autumn, and they are glorious as cut blooms. There is a rich vein from which to make a selection, but you have to be a little careful. The *H. macrophylla* varieties, embracing both hortensia and lacecaps, do not like a strongly limy soil. One of the best of these is 'Hamburg', which is normally a deep pink, but will be a rich blue on a fairly acid soil; its flowers last well into autumn. *H. mariesii* is a lacecap, with very large pink flowers, and one of the most spectacular is *H. villosa*, a bi-coloured blue/lavender, which seems to keep its colour in whatever soil it is grown.

### Hypericum St John's wort

Hypericum is wonderful for ground cover, especially *H. calycinum*, or rose of Sharon. This has almost everything you could want: deep green foliage, splendid yellow flowers, dense and quite rapid carpet-style growth – and it is evergreen. It flowers in early summer, and is followed by *H. elatum* 'Elstead', whose later yellow flowers appear as the first ones have set bright red seed pods. (See also page 85.)

### Ilex Holly

This is, of course, an evergreen. Not all carry berries, and a few are not prickly. Berries are invariably on female plants, and an oddity of nomenclature is that the 'Golden King' variety

Right: The delicate-flowered jasmine is treasured for its perfume. The common jasmine, *J. officinale*, is a climber that bears fine white blooms from June till September, given a fairly sheltered position.

Below: Old-fashioned it may be, but there are still few sights that bring greater pleasure than a border of lavender. The delicate hues, and the delightful cottage-garden fragrance, make lavender an enduring favourite. *Lavandula spica* is the traditional 'Mitcham' blue; it is also known as *L. angustifolia*.

is female and 'Golden Queen' is a male, with only green-grey and yellow leaves to give it regal distinction.

**Jasminum** Jasmine
One of our sweetest-scented climbers. *J. nudiflorum* is the winter jasmine, with bright yellow bell-like flowers showing around Christmas time; *J. officinale* is the white-flowered summer version.

**Lavandula** Lavender
This is a low-growing shrub, especially useful as a border plant, and traditional for lining a cottage garden. You can use it in clumps in a border or along a wall. It will accept poor, dry soil and in fact welcomes a sunny and warm spot. It is essentially a midsummer plant, and shows only slight variations of colour. *L. spica* is the traditional 'Mitcham' blue.

**Lonicera** Honeysuckle
How fortunate we are in the number of our perfumed shrubs! Although the honeysuckle is renowned for its summer perfume – not unlike that of azalea – it is not well enough known that

Left: Treasured among the hedgerows and also in the garden is the honeysuckle, or woodbine. The one shown is the hybrid *Lonicera × tellmanniana* — a notable climber that bestows its rich perfume for a month or so in the height of summer. Its rich golden blooms flourish up to about 6m (20ft).

Below: The berries of *Mahonia aquifolium* — good for jam-making.

there is a very fragrant winter-flowering variety, *L. purpusii*: short-growing, with white flowers. Best of the climbers is surely *L. periclymenum*, the common honeysuckle or woodbine that is a feature of the hedgerows for three months in summer. There are some hybrids, one of the best of which is *L. tellmanniana*, with huge clusters of good-sized flowers; it prefers some shade.

## Magnolia × soulangiana
Magnificent waxy white blooms, with a lemony perfume: a most gracious early-flowering shrub. Try to give it some protection: I have

seen twenty or thirty blooms ruined overnight by one of those treacherous spring frosts. *M. stellata*, slightly smaller, is even earlier with glorious freely-borne white blooms in March.

## Mahonia aquifolium Oregon grape
This one likes some shade. It produces bright yellow flowers in and around March and 'grapes' in autumn, when you may also get some foliage colour. An evergreen.

## Olearia Daisy bush
A really tough evergreen, so named because of its small daisy-like flowers: a good seaside plant

that also makes up into a fine hedge. Flowers appear in late summer.

### Paeonia
This is the tree paeony, the shrubby version of the perennial. It thrives in limy soil. Try *P. lutea ludlowii*, which has beautiful yellow flowers in spring.

### Parthenocissus Virginia creeper
A lovely, almost universal, climber that brings such richness to house walls as summer nears its end. *P. quinquefolia* is nominally self-clinging, but I have found that a little help in the early stages enables it to get away much faster.

### Philadelphus Mock orange
This is often wrongly called syringa (which is lilac). It has sweet-scented flowers, mainly white or cream. One of the most attractive is *P. microphyllus*, a dwarf growing to about 1m (3ft) and bearing white flowers in profusion.

### Pieris
An attractive evergreen. There are several varieties, some with red foliage in spring. They are distinguished by their lily of the valley flowers; very fragrant, and one of the most welcome of all spring-flowering plants. Most of them bloom in April; *P. taiwanensis* may show bloom in March.

### Potentilla
This is sometimes known as the shrubby cinquefoil, because its flowers have five circular petals. It is almost without exception yellow-flowered, running in succession from May to October. It makes an excellent low-growing border shrub, seldom above 1m (3ft) high. *P. fruticosa grandiflora* and *P. fruticosa* 'Katherine Dykes' are good for hedges. (See also page 78.)

### Pyracantha Firethorn
One of the most spectacular climbing shrubs, its great falls of vivid red berries showing up vividly against any wall. It has pleasant cream flowers in spring, but the effect of these is insignificant compared with the berries.

### Rhododendron
This is a large family, which includes azaleas and rhodoras. Varieties can be either deciduous or evergreen and tall or very low-growing. They all like damp soil and shade. *R. praecox* is a dwarf which flowers early. 'Pink Pearl', a famous and rather large bloom in the 'orthodox'

Above: The daisy bush, olearia, which gets its common name from its tight clusters of small, scented, daisy-like flowers.

Left: Dainty, small-leaved *Philadelphus microphyllus*.

Opposite: Virginia creeper, *Parthenocissus quinquefolia*.

Below: Pyracantha, the firethorn, provides a good display of creamy-white flowers in spring, but it is the summer and autumn berries that make it so striking.

hybrid range, comes a little later and there is a flood of them from May onwards. Azaleas come at about the same time with their haunting sweet fragrance. All hate lime, but the dwarfs can be grown in tubs.

### Rhus

Notable as a foliage shrub, with some striking red-yellow and orange effects from midsummer. Not very tall, mostly under 2m (6ft). *R. cotinus* is known as the smoke plant because of its feathery flower formation. *R. typhina*, the stag's horn sumach, is frequently sold as a tree, and a fast-growing one.

### Sambucus Elder

A familiar but underrated shrub which is a fine source of flowers and berries for wine. A fast grower, it will quickly reach 4m (12ft).

### Syringa Lilac

An old garden favourite, seen almost everywhere in May and June. It prefers chalk, but will survive happily in most soils, and does best in a sunny spot. Mainly white or purple, it is strongly perfumed. *S. vulgaris*, the common lilac, is said to be the parent of more hybrids than any other shrub: about 500.

### Tamarix Tamarisk

This is a rather straggly, feathery plant, delicate and graceful, but delicate only in appearance, for it is one of the most doughty resisters of seaside gales and spray. It grows to 2m (6ft) and

has masses of small pink flowers. To prevent it becoming too straggly, cut hard back in spring. *T. pentandra* is about the best of the dozen or so varieties available.

### Viburnum

One of the greatest of our entire range, both in numbers and attraction. Between them they offer flowers and/or berries and/or perfume all the year round. Some reach 2m (6ft). *V. opulus* is also known as the guelder rose. Beautiful white scented flowers in late spring give place in autumn to clusters of red berries and maple-colour foliage. It is also known as the water elder because it thrives in a damp situation.

*V. × burkwoodii*, one of the first to bloom, provides fragrant pink-white flowers in May. It is an evergreen. *V. tinus* is another evergreen, producing pinkish-white flowers in winter. *V. davidii*, a good all-the-year-rounder, is also evergreen, with summer flowers and frequently blue berries in winter.

### Wisteria

Last, but by no means least, in this section. Who has not gasped in admiration at the sight of an old house covered with its lovely blue blooms in early summer? Essentially a climber, it can reach between 6 and 9m (20 and 30ft) quite comfortably. Best known is probably *W. sinensis*, the Chinese wisteria, with fragrant deep blue or mauve flowers. Plant one at the front of your house and you will increase its selling value immediately!

## Conifers

So far I have made no mention of the two greatest classes of the shrub world. The reason simply is that they are so comprehensive that they deserve a special section to themselves. One is flowering, the other not. Roses and conifers, by the vastness of their scope, could fill many pages in any book, and still leave a lot unsaid.

In the broadest of terms, and for everyday purposes (though botanists would undoubtedly shoot down this rule-of-thumb description) conifers are those (mainly) green-leaved plants, trees and shrubs that provide leaf colour more or less all the year round, but are never seen in flower. Many of them will tower to thirty metres or more, and clearly are outside the scope of the ordinary gardener: they are specimens intended to take their place in a large natural 'mural', where the eye is invited to take in everything in sight over an area that may be a mile or more wide. For our purposes we are concentrating on plants for the garden, not the park, and anything that grows more than about ten metres high is therefore taboo. Here, first, are three personal favourites.

**Araucaria** Monkey puzzle tree
This was very popular a couple of generations ago, with its long, descending, twisting 'tails', and can still be seen quite frequently, which may be a tribute to its longevity. Theoretically, it can grow well above ten metres, but I cannot recall seeing one above bedroom height. It is slow-growing and, although well known and unforgettable because of its shape, comes into the category of 'good fun' plants. Officially, it is a tall-growing conifer, but don't be put off by that. It is evergreen, extremely symmetrical and does not mind fairly damp conditions, but is not really happy in a town (which, oddly, is where I seem to have seen most of them).

**Cedrus** Cedar
You can even have a cedar in quite a small garden. Try *C. deodar*, the Himalayan cedar, said to be the most graceful of them all. Yes, it does grow very large, but if you plant one now and move house in ten years' time it will have grown at most 4·5m (15ft) and you will have had all those years of distinction in your garden.

**Ginkgo biloba** Maidenhair tree
This is one of the oldest trees in existence: fossilized remains have been found, said to be

millions of years old, and there is only one type. It is of upright growth, notable for its fan-like leaves which turn yellow in autumn, and it grows almost anywhere. It is a very graceful tree, but one I had had been vandalized by a previous owner, who had cut off all the lower branches. I think he wanted it to be a focal point breaking up the line of a hedge, but it ruined the appearance of the tree.

The ginkgo is trouble-free , extremely distinctive, and will add a touch of 'something extra' to your garden. Although a number of nurseries stock it, it does seem to be rare in gardens. Nevertheless, it is easily obtainable. I am told that San Francisco and several other American cities plant them as roadside trees, much as London plants plane trees. They are certainly much more picturesque, and I am certain they are just as hardy.

This still leaves scores of more or less 'everyday' items from which to choose, and you cannot go wrong, for they all have a special beauty of their own. Virtually all are evergreen, and everything in the conifer domain is notable for the neatness of its shape, its close-knit foliage, its restful colourings in many shades of green, yellow and blue, plus, in many cases, that refreshing piney tang of the perfume. Breathe deeply and feel it is doing you good!

## Chamaecyparis

The lawsonianas dominate this section. 'Ellwoodii' is reasonably dwarf at 3m (10ft) and is blue-grey in colour. *Minima aurea* is a beauty in miniature: gold, and growing to barely 60cm (2ft), and is recommended for the rockery. That bright gold foliage is a picture, providing the perfect foil to almost everything else you have growing there. Very slow-growing.

## Cupressocyparis leylandii Cypress

The fastest-growing conifer we have, fully capable of rising at least 60cm (2ft) a year. If you are worried about this, it does stop growing after about fifteen years, at around 12m (40ft), but of course it can be kept down to more manageable proportions if you wish.

The best plan is to use it as a hedge – it will be a dense one. A brand new form, 'Castlewellan', which has a beautiful golden sheen, also grows quite fast, and is especially bright in the early months of the year. I think it will catch on and be very popular indeed within a few years. The old standby, privet, especially the golden privet, has its uses, but is a greedy feeder, and

stops almost everything else from growing anywhere near it. This one is much more decorative.

## Juniperus Juniper

One of the largest of the conifer 'families', notable for its aromatic foliage and its grey-green berries. In its many forms it shows all types of growth, but the foliage is poisonous to cattle. The junipers offer a range from prostrate low-growing forms to tall columns. One of the most popular, and only moderately tall, but narrow, is *J. communis hibernica*, the Irish juniper, with silvery-green foliage, rising to a little over 4m (12ft). *J. c. suecica*, the Swedish juniper, is similar in height and form, but the branches droop gracefully at the tips.

*J. c. compressa* is effectively a miniature Irish juniper, for it is unlikely to rise much above

### Taxus Yew

This is renowned for slow and steady growth. It is inevitably associated with churchyards, but I doubt whether its funereal pace has anything to do with it. Its other claim to fame is that it is toxic to cattle that try to eat it, but we assume you won't have that problem! Of all the hedging plants, I would say this is the most rewarding for a hedge-trimming expert to get his shears on: some wonderfully straight sides and edges can be achieved, mainly because of its tight, thick growth. *T. baccata* is the traditional English yew – no need to remind you what a wonderful hedge it makes. *T. fastigiata* is the Irish equivalent, growing slightly taller if allowed to.

### Thuya

(Sometimes spelt *Thuja.*) This one conforms more closely than most of the others to the conical shape from which conifers take their name. It is also surprisingly fragrant. *T. plicata* is notable as a hedging plant, but this and the many other varieties will easily stand on their own as specimen plants on a lawn or in borders. Normally they reach about 3m (10ft) but there are dwarf forms, one of the best being *T.* 'Rheingold', which forms a nicely-rounded golden-yellow bush about 1·5m (4ft) high – a very pleasant sight on a drab winter's day!

This can be only a very brief resumé of the best known of the hundreds of conifers available. Apart from the garden centres, which, like me, can deal with only a few, there are several specialist nurseries which it is both an education and a pleasure to visit: you will be surprised at the vast range.

Left: *Taxus baccata*, the common or English yew, easily trims into a fine hedge; the close leafy texture forms an impenetrable barrier.

Below: Thuyas normally grow to 3m (10ft). This one, *T. occidentalis* 'Rheingold', a beautiful golden variety, is a comparative dwarf, only about 1½m (5ft).

60cm (2ft) and is ideal for the rock garden. *J. horizontalis* – there are several forms – is exactly what it says, forming a thick mat only 30cm (1ft) or even less above the ground, and is perfect for hiding unsightly items like drains and manhole covers. The *J. squamatas* – again in several forms – are also low and spreading but slightly taller, up to about 1m (3ft).

### Larix Larch

This is, believe it or not, a conifer, though it is deciduous. It grows quickly and will reach 5m (16ft) in a few years, but the green and yellow foliage will be a welcome sight in the meantime.

Left: The Himalayan juniper is a magnificent specimen, and really needs a large and well-matured garden to do it justice, for it will eventually grow to 15m (50ft) or more. The foliage of this one, *J. recurva coxii*, droops gracefully — hence its common name, drooping juniper.

# 5 Roses Old and New

## The universal favourites

Shakespeare was, of course, absolutely correct when he declared that a rose by any other name would smell as sweet. The only doubt is whether whatever other name it had would roll so melodiously off the tongue. As a cut bloom it is unsurpassed; there is, in fact, a vast industry specializing in roses purely for that purpose. It is also the most popular of all our garden inhabitants, and small wonder. The blooms offer so much pleasure for so little. There is no monotony about them; indeed, in many cases there are bonuses of distinctive leaf colouring and, at the end of the flowering season, a magnificent display of heps: the seed pods or fruits.

They will tolerate most conditions other than waterlogging, baulking only at extreme clay and extreme chalk. Indeed they will thrive in conditions no plant might be expected to endure. They will also offer bloom from June or July (perhaps earlier) to near Christmas, sometimes beyond if the weather is kind. All they ask in return is to be kept neat and tidy and well fed, with occasional checks, and for years to come they will go on supplying you with beautifully-coloured, delicate-looking, but extremely tough blooms that will bring delight and probably perfume to the garden and, if cut, will enhance the appearance of any room indoors.

Also in their favour is that they are not fastidious as to how they are grown. You can grow them singly – in pots, if you like, having no garden handy and only a balcony – as standards on a lawn, or in beds or borders grouped together. Some varieties make picturesque hedges, odorous and pretty impenetrable.

Then, too, they come in so many forms, in size and habit of growth. The bush types are the most widely used and the best suited to beds and borders. The standards, useful as single specimens or to 'landscape' a bed by giving extra height, are versions of the bush types: the same flowers but grown on different stock,

producing a single and usually taller main stem. There are climbers, ramblers, ground cover – low-growing but spreading to cover a diameter of 5m (16ft) or more – and miniatures, tiny versions growing barely 15cm (6in) high, making excellent border plants and possibly (because they require so little space) having a great future in these days of small gardens and small growing areas.

Contrasting with these are the old-fashioned, simply-styled, shrub roses, though some are of modern raising. Some of them, if not kept well trimmed, can grow rather large and it is as well to respect their individuality by being generous with space and allotting them more than the normal 1m (3ft) maximum between plants.

But this is only the start: you still have a choice of type of bloom. Hybrid teas and floribundas easily lead the poll because between

Left: Yellow roses and yellow-flowered lysimachia with the blue and white platycodon.

Below: 'Henri Martin', one of the loveliest of the old moss roses, bears heavily-petalled crimson flowers and grows to about 2m (7ft).

them they provide colour for so many months and because there are many more varieties. But many a discerning gardener has one or two of the old-fashioned shrub roses (with ancestry centuries old) which, although they generally have a restricted flowering period, offer a grace and form – and often subtle perfume – that the modern versions cannot touch.

You may murmur a critical comment that roses are thorny, and so offer a deterrent to admirers who approach too close. But you can get roses without thorns, though admittedly there are not very many, and this could be a profitable area for an adventurous breeder to explore. Nevertheless, 'Zéphirine Drouhin', best known of the thornless ones, has been popular for well over a hundred years. It is a deep pink scented climber that lasts and lasts and whose only fault may be a susceptibility to mildew, a fault by no means confined to this variety. *Rosa rubrifola*, a species growing up to 2·5m (7½ft) or more, is almost thornless.

## History of the Rose

The rose has a history as long and confusing as life itself. Fossilized remains, estimated at more than three million years old, are said to have been of *R. damascena*, the damask rose. But some historians claim that the damask is a descendant of *R. alba*, which traditionally is white but has a disconcerting knack of sometimes appearing pink (hence its other names of the 'White Rose of York' and 'Maiden's Blush').

The truth is that nobody really knows much about the origin of the rose. All we can say with certainty is that roses grew wild and flourished throughout most areas of the world many thousands of years ago and there is no sign that we are growing tired of them yet.

Indeed, the art of rose cultivation is a comparatively modern one, only two or three centuries old, so we have much to learn from and about the rose. This may explain an impelling urge to produce new varieties, new strains, new colours to meet the public demand for something new and spectacular every year. Always, or almost always, there is at least one new variety clearly destined to earn fame and fortune, but it must be admitted that every year also there are some newcomers that have only novelty and a different name to distinguish them from others just as good.

### The Old Shrub Rose

We still have with us over a hundred of the old-type species rose, and these are always catalogued and named with the prefix *Rosa*. They were, broadly, the first of the cultivated roses, but cultivated in a rarer, more leisurely, atmosphere of graciousness and spaciousness. The *Rosa* prefix is an accolade of distinction, segregating them from the mass-produced, florists' types we grow and know under the common name of rose.

Many a large garden has one or more of them,

but they are worth a place anywhere if you are prepared to allow them living room: 2m (6ft) square and high. They are generally referred to as shrub roses, and their descendants as modern shrub roses. The characteristics of some of the best known of them are worth mentioning, for they have had a great influence on the breeding of virtually all the roses in commerce today.

The old roses differ from the modern bush plants in the formation of the flowers. Mostly they are just single petals or what are known as semi-double: a further layer of petals more or less alternating, but often providing little more than a dozen in all. They open quickly and stay open for their short life. Compare that with the thirty or more petals of most modern roses, which hold their bud form for some days and do not open to reveal their inner secrets until they are on the point of going over.

I mentioned *R. damascena* as being one of the oldest. This is a semi-double, varying from white to red, and intensely fragrant (the petals

Information chart 6 ROSES

### TWELVE FOR PERFUME

| | | | |
|---|---|---|---|
| Albertine | pink | cl/ramb | prolific |
| Alec's Red | scarlet | ht | large-flowered |
| Dearest | pink | fl | vigorous |
| Elizabeth of Glamis | salmon pink | fl | free-flowering |
| Ena Harkness | crimson | ht | long-lasting bloom |
| Escapade | pink/violet | fl | semi-double flowers |
| Fragrant Cloud | orange/scarlet | ht | large leaves |
| Josephine Bruce | deep red | ht | vigorous grower |
| Margaret Merril | white/pink | fl | very fragrant |
| Sutter's Gold | orange/yellow | ht | prolific |
| Tenerife | pink/orange | ht | very fragrant |
| Wendy Cussons | cerise/pink | ht | free-flowering |

### TWELVE FOR CUTTING

| | | | |
|---|---|---|---|
| Blue Moon | lavender/lilac | ht | fragrant |
| Ena Harkness | crimson | ht | fragrant, long-lasting |
| Fragrant Cloud | orange/scarlet | ht | very fragrant |
| Frensham | crimson | fl | tall growth |
| *R. gallica versicolor* (*Rosa mundi*) | pink/purple | shrub | attractive striping |
| Iceberg | white | fl | profuse flowering |
| Just Joey | copper/orange | ht | red-tinged leaves |
| Queen Elizabeth | soft pink | fl | dark foliage ; slight fragrance |
| Red Devil | deep scarlet | ht | fragrant; long-lasting |
| Rose Gaujard | white/pink/ silver | ht | long-lasting |
| Southampton | apricot | fl | fragrant; unusual colour |
| Sutter's Gold | orange/yellow | ht | free-flowering; well-shaped |

### TWELVE REDS

| | | | |
|---|---|---|---|
| Alec's Red | scarlet | ht | fragrant, large-flowered |
| City of Belfast | deep scarlet | fl | disease-resistant |
| Ernest H. Morse | crimson | ht | fragrant |
| Frensham | crimson | fl | vigorous; mildew-prone |
| Heidelberg | crimson | shrub | also a pillar climber |
| Josephine Bruce | deep red | ht | fragrant, but has weak neck |
| News | purple | fl | free-flowering |
| Parkdirektor Riggers | deep crimson | cl | long flowering season |
| Red Devil | deep scarlet | ht | strong grower |
| Super Star | vermilion | ht | fragrant |
| Topsi | scarlet | fl | dwarf-growing ; good for borders |
| Wendy Cussons | cerise/pink | ht | fragrant |

## TWELVE PINK/ORANGE/APRICOT

| | | | |
|---|---|---|---|
| Beauté | orange apricot | ht | profuse flowering |
| Elizabeth of Glamis | salmon pink | fl | fragrant |
| Escapade | pink/violet | fl | subtle perfume |
| Evelyn Fison | orange/scarlet | fl | vigorous; serrated edges |
| Just Joey | copper/orange | ht | red-tinged foliage |
| Mischief | salmon pink | ht | fragrant; good bedding rose |
| Orange Sensation | orange/vermilion | fl | fragrant |
| Pink Favourite | deep pink | ht | disease-resistant |
| Queen Elizabeth | soft pink | fl | tall-growing |
| Schoolgirl | apricot/orange | cl | fragrant |
| Southampton | apricot | fl | disease-resistant |
| Whisky Mac | orange | ht | fragrant |

## TWELVE YELLOW/CREAM/WHITE

| | | | |
|---|---|---|---|
| Allgold | yellow/gold | fl | disease-resistant |
| Arthur Bell | yellow/cream | fl | fragrant |
| Buccaneer | deep yellow | ht | good for border |
| Canary Bird | pure yellow | sp | fragrant |
| Chinatown | yellow/pink | fl/shrub | fragrant |
| Frau Karl Druschki | white | ht | vigorous; weather-resistant |
| Goya | white | ht/fl | fragrant |
| Iceberg | white | fl | tall-growing |
| King's Ransom | golden yellow | ht | vigorous |
| Pascali | white | ht | free-flowering |
| Peace | yellow/pink | ht | very vigorous |
| Sunsilk | yellow | fl | large flowers, good for cutting |

## TWELVE BI-COLOURS

| | | | |
|---|---|---|---|
| Bonfire Night | scarlet/gold | fl | good for cutting |
| Caramba | crimson/silver | ht | very thorny |
| Daily Sketch | pink/silver | fl | fragrant |
| Esther Ofarim | red/orange/yellow | fl | short, heavy-bearing, bush |
| Eye Paint | red/white centre | fl | eye-catching open flowers |
| R. gallica versicolor (Rosa mundi) | pink/purple stripe | shrub | very strong |
| Harry Wheatcroft | scarlet/yellow | ht | attractive striping |
| Isabel de Ortiz | pink/silver | ht | fragrant |
| Masquerade | yellow/pink/red | fl | dead-head for repeat flowering |
| Piccadilly | scarlet/yellow | ht | free-flowering |
| Pineapple Poll | yellow/scarlet | fl | unusual sharp perfume |
| Tzigane | scarlet/yellow | ht | copper foliage |

## SIX BLUES

| | | | |
|---|---|---|---|
| Blue Moon | lavender/lilac | ht | very fragrant |
| Harry Edland | lilac | fl | very fragrant |
| Lagoon | lilac | fl | green/copper foliage |
| Ripples | lilac/mauve | fl | frilled petals |
| Silver Charm | lavender | fl | fragrant |
| Sterling Silver | mauve | ht | fragrant |

## TWELVE CLIMBERS AND RAMBLERS

| | | | |
|---|---|---|---|
| Albéric Barbier | yellow/cream | ramb | profuse flowering |
| Albertine | pink | ramb | very vigorous |
| Compassion | pink/orange | cl | fragrant |
| Danse du Feu | orange/scarlet | cl | free-flowering |
| Golden Showers | orange/yellow | cl | fragrant; long-lasting |
| Maigold | orange/gold | cl | very fragrant; hardy |
| Parkdirektor Riggers | deep crimson | cl | hardy; long-flowering |
| Paul's Scarlet Climber | scarlet | cl | an old favourite; slightly scented |
| Pink Perpétue | pink | cl/ramb | glossy dark green leaves |
| Schoolgirl | apricot/orange | cl | fragrant |
| Swan Lake | white/pink | cl | weather-resistant |
| Zéphirine Drouhin | pink | cl | fragrant; thornlesss |

## TWELVE FOR HEDGES

| | | | |
|---|---|---|---|
| Dorothy Wheatcroft | orange | fl | very vigorous |
| *R. eglanteria* Lady Penzance | copper/pink | sp | one of the sweet briars |
| Escapade | pink/violet | fl | vigorous |
| Frensham | crimson | fl | tall growth |
| Frühlingsgold | yellow | h/shrub | fragrant |
| Heidelberg | crimson | cl/shrub | strong growth |
| Iceberg | white | fl | vigorous; fragrant |
| Masquerade | yellow/pink/red | fl | vigorous |
| Nevada | cream/pink | h/shrub | thick thorns; free-flowering |
| Penelope | cream/pink | h/musk | splendid in autumn |
| Queen Elizabeth | soft pink | fl | tall; free-flowering |
| *R. rugosa scabrosa* | mauve/pink | sp | fragrant; good heps |

## TWELVE AUTUMN SPECIALISTS (notable for heps)

| | | |
|---|---|---|
| *R. canina* | | large orange-scarlet oval heps |
| Frau Dagmar Hastrup | | pink flowers, large crimson heps, fragrant |
| *R. davidii* | | elongated bristly heps |
| *R. helenae* | | small oval heps |
| *R. microphylla* | | green heps like horse chestnuts |
| *R. moyesii geranium* | | bright red flowers; large heps |
| *R. rubrifolia* | | red stems, almost thornless ; brownish red heps |
| *R. rugosa alba* | | round red heps, like small tomatoes |
| *R. rugosa rubra* | | round heps, golden foliage |
| *R. rugosa scabrosa* | | large orange-red heps, fragrant |
| *R. spinosissima* | | Scots briar : hardy, thorny ; large round black heps |
| *R. swegnziowii macrocarpa* | | very thorny ; bright red heps early in season |

## KEY

| | | |
|---|---|---|
| ht | — | hybrid tea |
| fl | — | floribunda |
| cl | — | climber |
| ramb | — | rambler |
| sp | — | species |
| h | — | hybrid |

# The rose garden: a choice of colours...

Roses are available in a wide range of beautiful colours. This guide to colour schemes suggests particularly successful combinations for a rose garden – one of the loveliest sights of the summer months.

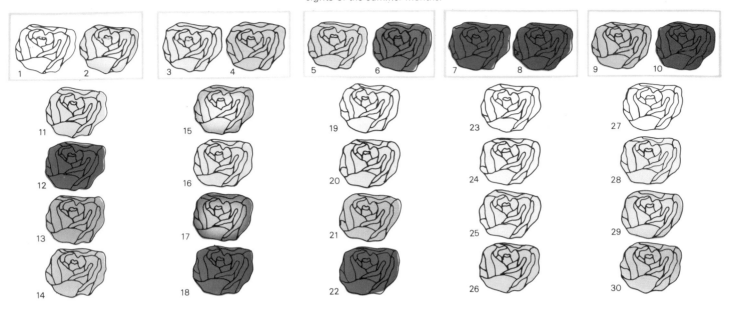

## How to use the colour guide

**Colours 1-10 The base colours.** Choose a basic colour from these: five pairs show the spectrum of rose colours, from pure white to deep crimson.
**Colours 11-30 The complementary colours.** These complement the base colours: the four colours in each column go well with shades of the base colours immediately above them (but not necessarily with each other).

## ..and four plans

The garden plans below suggest how many variations can be worked on this theme.

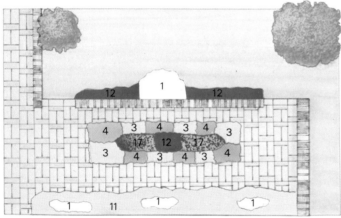

White and yellow are the basic shades in a simple design of bold, bright colours.

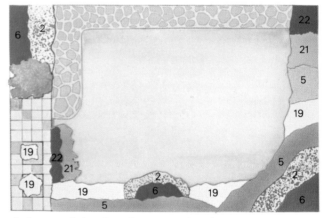

Delicate gradations from flame, through apricot, cream and a cream/apricot bi-colour, to soft pink and crimson.

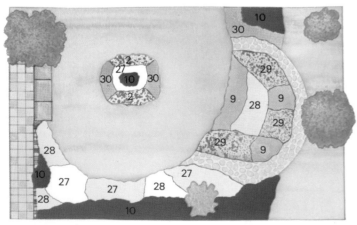

Deep crimson and strong pink are complemented by pale apricot and a pink/yellow bi-colour, and linked by neutral cream and white.

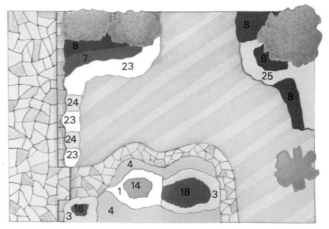

Bold colours combine well if the right shades are chosen. Here different schemes blend: deep red, scarlet, crimson and delicate purple are balanced by white, cream and two shades of yellow.

are used in making attar of roses). Best known of them is *R. d. versicolor*, which, because of its white and pink flowers, has become famous as the 'York and Lancaster' rose. *R. alba* ('Maiden's Blush'), has already been mentioned. Other favourites are *R. canina*, the dog rose of our hedges, white and pink, and *R. gallica versicolor*, with red and white stripes (some catalogues describe them as pink and purple, which – because this is more accurate in this writer's eye – is how they are described in the accompanying tables). This one is better known as *R. mundi*, supposedly honouring the mistress of King Henry II; it continues in flower longer than most of the others, often up to three months.

*R. centifolia*, popularly supposed to have a hundred petals, is known as the cabbage rose and it is not hard to see why, with its tightly packed rosettes, deep pink in colour. It is closely related to the moss rose, and they are usually listed together. One of the centifolias, 'Cristata', is known as the crested moss (another name is 'Chapeau de Napoleon') because of a peculiar 'cockade' over the bud.

The 'moss' is actually a series of tiny glands covering the flower stalks, and certainly imparts a distinctive appearance. One of the best known varieties of the moss rose is 'Henri Martin', over a hundred years old, heavily covered in rich crimson flowers and – naturally – delicately scented.

But for delicacy of perfume it would be hard to beat the musk rose. The original musk, *R. moschata*, is now very rarely found, and most of those available are hybrids (probably from the Himalayan musk). Two quite widely available are 'Felicia', salmon-pink/yellow, growing to about 1·5m (4½ft) and 'Ballerina', slightly smaller and dual-coloured in that the pink flower has an attractive white eye.

*R. moyesii*, another species rose, is quite a modern one, dating from the turn of the century, but earns its place in the gallery of rose immortals for the number and quality of its heps: large, bottle-shaped and bright orange, contrasting with the deep red of the flowers. *R. chinensis*, the China rose, (white to red) can bloom from midsummer till early autumn. There is even a greenish-flowered species,

Above: *Rosa canina*, the common dog rose, so prolific in the hedgerows. It is very vigorous, growing to 4m (13½ft).

Top: *Rosa gallica versicolor* (*R. mundi*), known from the 15th century, grows to 1½m (5ft).

Opposite: *Rosa rugosa*.
The rugosas are among the
oldest of the roses;
although they may be
surpassed in bloom by
the multi-petalled
brilliance of the modern
hybrid teas and floribundas,
they do have an attractive
single flower and in autumn
bear marvellous heps,
or seed pods. *R. rugosa* is little
grown now, but worth having.
The basis of many of the
standard roses, it is very
hardy and can be used for
hedges, growing to 3m (10ft).

Left: 'Pink Grootendorst',
one of the rugosas — a
prickly old-type shrub
rose but in fact a modern
(post-war) variety.
It grows to 1½m (5ft), is
pink in colour, and makes
a good vase rose.

Below: These long prickly
heps are the seeds
of *Rosa moyesii,* an
outstandingly beautiful
contribution to
the autumn scene.

*viridiflora*, and a series of miniatures, also descended from the versatile *chinensis*.

R. *rugosa*, the Ramanas rose, is red or white flowered, very fragrant, and also has bright scarlet heps. *R. wichuraiana*, which might be termed the parent of the ramblers, extends to about 4m (12ft) and has white flowers and dark glossy foliage. Finally there is the eglantine of *A Midsummer Night's Dream*, the sweet briar 'Eglanteria', which has pink flowers and heps and even the foliage smells sweet. Small wonder that Shakespeare enthused!

There are some excellent modern versions of these old species. 'Chinatown', a yellow-pink, sometimes described as a floribunda shrub, grows very strongly, filling the air with perfume, and seems to thrive in difficult circumstances. I once had to plant some bushes in unprepared ground at the start of a very dry summer, and they stood up to that torture far

better than any of the varieties growing nearby. The second flush is not as strongly perfumed as the first, but is still good enough, and as it grows to 2m (6ft) it can make its presence felt in no uncertain way.

Among other outstanding modern shrubs are 'Nevada', with large, single creamy white to pink blooms, and 'Heidelberg', a bright red. For a mixture of colour there is the aptly named 'Joseph's Coat' (yellow, orange and red) which makes a good climber, and 'Ballerina', the hybrid musk already mentioned, which is pink with a white eye.

One of the most aptly named of our roses is the species hybrid 'Canary Bird'. That should inspire a vision of fluttering yellow wings, and the spectacle of masses of small yellow flowers stretching the length of the stem comes very close to it. 'La Reine Victoria' is another close to the vision: a stately, solid Bourbon type – regal, even – with masses of tight pink petals.

So many excellent roses are in cultivation that no list I can offer would do more than just cover a small proportion. I have dealt here with some of the shrub roses by way of tribute to their ancestry and in the hope that it may encourage gardeners to venture away from the mono-polistic, though never monotonous, ring of hybrid teas and floribundas.

Above: 'Canary Bird' is a modern shrub; its early, free-flowering, single yellow blooms extend almost to the end of the 2½m (8ft) stem to form a dense pattern of buttercup-like colour. Like most shrubs it is freer from disease than the conventional hybrid teas and floribundas.

Right: 'Pink Perpétué', introduced in the mid-sixties, is one of the best of the modern climbers and is also classed as a rambler. Pink/carmine in colour, with free and continuous flowering till late in the season, it is good for walls or pillars, and grows to about 2½m (8ft).

## Hybrid Teas and Floribundas

The difference between these two, broadly, is that the hybrid teas are more or less pointed blooms growing singly on a stem; the flori-bundas, borne in clusters, are somewhat flatter in shape and tend to flower more continously. In general, hybrid teas are better-perfumed and floribundas stand up better to wet condi-tions. In terms of rose history they are both very modern, for the hybrid teas were un-known until about a century ago and 'flori-bunda', as a name, was not coined until after the last world war. Both are the result of prolific cross breeding. The hybrid teas came about by, it is said, a chance crossing of a hybrid perpetual with a tea rose (so called because the fragrance of this type resembled that of a newly-opened tea chest). Half a century later a hybrid tea in turn was crossed with a polyantha pompon rose, and the resultant seedling was classified as a hybrid polyantha.

The new type began to gain popularity in the 1930s and after the war further breeding and second-generation crosses involved more use of the hybrid teas. As the polyantha characteristics largely disappeared the name hybrid polyantha was felt to be anachronistic and the breed was called floribunda instead.

The story of the evolution of the modern rose is not finished yet and is taking a somewhat bizarre turn. For, responding to the impatient public's clamour for something new every year, breeders have tried more and more crosses, with the result that floribundas and hybrid teas are becoming so merged in their characteristics that we are now getting hybrid tea-shaped blooms growing in clusters. Even experts are admitting to difficulty in deciding whether some of the newcomers are hybrid teas or floribundas (some have been classed as both) and clearly another name is almost due.

There are so many varieties of rose, and so many ways of using them, that to recount them would be boringly repetitive, so I have included tables listing some of the main requirements a gardener may have and some of the best varieties for meeting them. The lists are a selection, far from complete, and may even draw criticism. But there are few sharply defined areas of demarcation in the world of the rose. Personal judgment, and growing conditions, must be the final arbiter.

Even the rose growers' catalogues, lavish and informative as most of them are, can mention

only a small proportion of the numbers that exist. They give a very fair representation of the colour, shape and characteristics of the varieties portrayed, but the best catalogue I know is a living one: the grounds of the Royal National Rose Society at St Albans, Hertfordshire, England. Here can be seen nearly 1,750 varieties (30,000 plants in all), giving a practical demonstration of what they are and what they

Above: 'Iceberg': probably the most popular white floribunda ever raised. Below left: *Rosa rugosa* and its hybrids are notable for the fine tomato-shaped heps that take over from the blooms. Below right: The Royal National Rose Society's grounds at St Albans.

139

One of the best of all modern roses is 'Peace', with its wonderfully healthy foliage and lush blossoms. The paved path is lined with grey-leaved *Stachys lamata* and nepeta.

can do. You can see new ones on trial and not yet available for purchase (some of them not even named), a parade of top award winners of past years, and beds, borders, walls, pergolas and pillars covered with blooms in the situations for which they are best suited. If you cannot find here the variety you want, I have no doubt that the enthusiastic officers and staff will do their utmost to trace a source of supply of the one you feel you must have.

I feel that two hybrid teas deserve a special mention, however, because of the great part they have played in the post-war history of the rose. One is 'Peace'; the other 'Super Star'. But although so closely connected, they could scarcely be more dissimilar. 'Peace' owes its position as the outstanding rose of our time not so much to its perfection as a rose as to the inspiration that gave it its name – it began life in France as 'Mme A. Meilland' and was renamed in America to mark the end of the Second World War. 'Super Star', from Germany, and almost twenty years younger, is the fiery fluorescent red that made such a striking colour

breakthrough: it is called 'Tropicana' in America.

The irony is that 'Peace' was one of the 'grandparents' – Tantau, the raiser, apparently was not sure about some of the others. No matter: 'Super Star' has established its own pedigree. The newer versions seem to be mellowing and losing some of the early fire (one leading grower is actually describing it as orange!) and there are reports that it is also more susceptible as a breed to mildew than it was. But whatever its fate it deserves, and will hold, a prominent place in the recent history of the rose.

'Peace' is claimed to be the most popular rose that has ever been produced. This probably means that more trees of it have been sold than any other variety. One estimated total marking the silver jubilee of its introduction was 100 million. Undoubtedly it was given a tremendous boost because of the name bestowed on it by a marketing genius at a time of great national and international emotion. It is a yellow, tinged with pink. Some experts downpoint it because

Two of the best roses of summer growing together — 'Golden Showers' and the vivid red 'Super Star'.

of failure to hold its shape: it 'blows' quickly and tends to look rather untidy. But on one point it does earn top marks. It is one of the two healthiest roses at present known to man. ('Pink Favourite', also a hybrid tea, is the other.)

Apart from all their attributes as garden flowers, roses lend themselves enthusiastically to experiments in hybridization. Crossing roses is, assuming you have the patience and the equipment (summed up as a camel-hair brush and a score or so of different varieties), one of the easiest and most satisfying ways of playing with Nature.

The emasculating and pollinating process is such that in a breeding house or shed one solitary plant can be showing a dozen or more blooms, all different in colour and shape, and all from the crosses that their owner has made. Anyone can do it, and thousands of new blooms are produced every year, many of them by amateurs. Very few are better than those already in existence, but there is always the chance of a freak or sport. The hope of producing another 'Peace' or another 'Super Star', though remote, will always be prominent in a breeder's mind.

The bewildering extent of the range explains simultaneously why the rose has so many adherents and why it must be placed in a special category away from those 'lesser breeds' of shrub. (In passing, professional rose growers invariably refer to their roses as 'trees', so you must draw your own conclusions!)

## Planning a Rose Garden

### Soil
You do not need a vast area to set up your rose garden: you could, if necessary, get a striking display from a border. All you need is a fairly sunny position, well drained and if possible well manured soil, and for preference neither pure clay nor pure chalk.

### Making the Plan
Almost certainly the bulk of your display will be a bed or two of bushes (in other words, the non-standards, the non-climbers, the non-ramblers,

etc). They will delight you with a glorious first flush. With many, after a few weeks the blooms will die away and the bushes will have a rest (do your part then by removing the spent blooms), coming back with a second crop in late summer or early autumn that will continue until the mists and frosts signal the end of the year.

A common mistake, however, especially by new gardeners, is failure to realize the improvement that can be effected in a rose bed by having blooms at different levels. So have one or more standards, dotted about here and there. As I have explained, these are mainly some of the popular hybrid tea and floribunda varieties grown on different stock producing a longer single stem, so you should be able to smell the perfume at head height instead of having to bend!

You can get them as full standards, approximately 1·3m (4ft) high, or half standards, about 1m (3ft). There are taller ones, very graceful, as they take a weeping or pendulous form, and these are an adaptation of the rambler. An avenue of standards on either side of a path makes a very impressive show. Alternatively, you could have a tiered effect in a bed with a row of weeping standards at the back, hiding the fence, with full standards in the

middle and a row of half standards at the front.

A further variation on the height theme is provided by dwarf or miniature versions. These are ideal for the front of any border: perfect scaled-down specimens that take up little room but give a lot of pleasure. The only cautionary point is that the soil around them must be kept well clear, for they can easily be smothered by rampant neighbours and can so easily be lost to view. 'Baby Masquerade', which has an ever-changing colour scheme, is a good one for this purpose.

There is another low-growing category, not very widely used but tremendously effective, especially if you have a fair amount of room. There are certain roses that are ground-cover specialists: they reach a height of barely 45cm (1½ft) but spread themselves over a diameter of about 5m (16ft). Their long rambling stems need pegging down, and in the early stages of growth their appearance is a little sparse. But soon their domain is covered with leaf, and then hundreds of small flowers appear, forming a glorious low dome of colour. A comparatively new one, and one of the best, is called 'Nozomi', a Japanese variety that has masses of small pink flowers and seemingly thousands of tiny leaves. It can be trained up or along a wall, but it looks marvellous as a low dome a metre or more in diameter.

By contrast, and providing yet a further dimension, you can have climbers and ramblers. For this purpose you need a wall or fence. Old apple trees are also favourite sites. And such is the versatility of the rose that there is one species, *R. wichuraiana*, that has a hand in both low-growing ground cover and high-rise climbing varieties.

*R. wichuraiana* is one of our oldest roses and rose types. It can be used as a shrub (white single flowers open mid- to late summer) or pinned down as a ground-cover specimen. It is also parent of a number of climbers and ramblers: 'American Pillar' among the climbers, and 'Albéric Barbier', 'Albertine' and 'Dorothy Perkins' being perhaps the best known among the ramblers.

Climbers and ramblers so closely resemble each other that a short identification may be useful. Generally, the ramblers are of trailing habit (the rambler-type standards, with their weeping style, make ideal specimens to enhance the appearance of a fairly large lawn), producing flowering shoots every year from the base. These bloom abundantly for three weeks or so and then die, and the old wood has to be cut

'Blue Moon': blue roses are not very popular, probably because there is not yet a true blue, though most of them are fragrant. 'Blue Moon', a hybrid tea regarded as the nearest to true blue yet, is actually a lavender/lilac mixture. It is the successor to 'Sterling Silver' (one of its parents), has a perfume, holds its colour well, and is particularly good as a cut flower. It grows to 1m (3ft).

away at the base every year to allow the new shoots to develop.

The climbers, which on the whole provide a longer flowering period, do not renew from the base but from higher up the stem. This means that the canes are sturdier than those of the rambler, and experience has shown that while the climber is ideal for training up a wall or fence, the ramblers are happier doing just that, trailing over, and covering, convenient open spaces.

But there are exceptions. The lovely fragrant pink 'Albertine' will willingly shoot up the side of a sunny wall, turning many a house or cottage exterior into a picture long before most of the other roses are out. One very useful climber is 'Maigold', a fragrant bronze-yellow beauty that thrives on a north wall, flowers early and prolifically, and seems remarkably free from the diseases that afflict most roses from time to time. But it has vicious thorns – a striking contrast to the thornless climber 'Zéphirine Drouhin' already mentioned.

Finally, if you have a fairly big area you can devote to your rose garden, you must have some of the old shrub roses to complete the picture. These are really the old masters. By modern standards their blooms may be small, almost

A flourishing rose garden with floribunda 'Iceberg' and 'Evelyn Fison' at the front, and climbers 'Golden Showers' and 'Chaplin's Pink' at the back.

insignificant perhaps, but they spread and make a wonderful sight as well as often conveying a delicious ethereal perfume. Moreover, they have stamina, in spite of the fact that generally they bloom for only a few weeks in the year. But go through a rose dictionary, or a connoisseur's catalogue, and you will find the old names cropping up again and again.

### Selecting

A healthy rose should last fifteen to twenty years or more, given reasonable conditions, so it is well worthwhile making sure you buy good quality roses to start with. Look for at least three strong shoots and good root development, and check that the rose is not too dry. This is particularly important if you buy roses that are pre-packed in polythene: the sort that may have been kept too long in the overheated atmosphere of a store.

### Preparation and Planting

Although roses demand very little attention, a little pre-arrival preparation will ensure good results. Because, to some extent, they are coarse feeders, a good helping of well rotted manure or compost in the bottom of the planting hole is the first requirement, but be careful that raw manure is not allowed to come into direct contact with the roots. Make sure, too, that the soil is well watered beforehand, and also that the plants themselves have been stood in water, preferably for twenty-four hours. If you plant the roots dry you suffer considerable delay before seeing your first blooms.

The soil mark on the bushes will be a good guide to planting depth, and see that the hole is wide enough for the roots to spread out in comfort. Bear in mind that each one has to go foraging through the soil for the food that will produce healthy blooms. The only way in which you must restrict them is by firming the soil thoroughly, partly to avoid air pockets and maintain close contact between root fibre and soil particles, but equally to prevent the plant blowing about in the wind, with consequent risk of damage or even uprooting. If you are planting standards, which need support, drive the stake into the soil first, making sure that it is firmly in position. A looped 'belt', figure-eight style, is the best way to secure the tree to the stake. The tie must not chafe the bark, while leaving enough room for expansion but not enough for movement. October to March is the best time for planting, but make sure the soil is not too wet for planting firmly.

Top: 'Danse du Feu' grows vigorously up to 3½m (12ft), with foliage changing colour from bronze to dark green.

Above: 'Albéric Barbier'. One of the best of the old-style climber/ramblers: yellow fading to white or cream, sweetly-scented, with ample flower and foliage and very vigorous, growing to 8m (27ft).

Right: 'Dorothy Perkins', an old favourite growing to 4m (13ft), and still one of the best for covering a pergola or screen.

## General Care

Roses demand little attention to keep them in good condition. They need pruning in spring, before growth starts, and dead-heading when the blooms are finished. They need feeding – normally with a good mulch of farm manure if possible, otherwise compost and a fairly regular liquid diet – and the occasional spray to take care of such annoyances as aphids and other pests, and diseases such as black spot and mildew. Also, both the appearance and condition of the rose bed will be improved if it is kept well weeded and the fallen leaves are removed, in case they harbour any spores of the various troubles that could overwinter in the soil and start up again early next year.

## Accompanying Plants

The one drawback about a rose bed is that it does look rather bare during those months when you are waiting for the buds to form and make you feel that summer really is on the way. For apart from the satisfaction of looking at neatly pruned trees (taken down to within a few centimetres of the ground in March, with the cut, if possible, about 1cm above an outward facing bud), there is nothing particularly inspiring about a rose bed with just a few twigs showing. Understandably many gardeners wish to have some other plant there to relieve the bareness of those early months of spring.

My own opinion is that it is a pity to detract from the glory of a bed of roses in full flower. From the practical aspect, roses do at all times need some attention, whether dead-heading, weeding, spraying, or just inspecting to make sure you can catch troubles at the outset. This obviously means that if you have to tread on the bed it is most inadvisable to have some other plant getting under your feet; ground-cover plants will make access difficult. Above all, since weeds do their utmost to invade and ruin the appearance of every well tended flower bed, the only treatment, short of constant hoeing, is weedkiller. Simazine is widely used, as is a paraquat/diquat formulation, which is harmless to the woody part of a shrub but plays havoc with anything green on which it is splashed.

If you wish to have your rose bed showing colour for as much of the year as possible, and dislike the use of weedkiller, your best approach is to have some springtime display that imparts its glory before the roses come on the scene and then meekly passes off stage. For early-year colour you won't go far wrong with snowdrops and crocuses, and the traditional lobelia and alyssum will provide a cheerful edging. There is a new red alyssum, called 'Wonderland', but it is so dark that it definitely needs a partner as a contrast. The golden-yellow *A. saxatile* is probably the favourite in the range.

One very useful stand-in is a display of wallflowers. Planted in autumn, they will provide their own distinctive colour and scent for many weeks from early spring till midsummer, taking you well into rose-blooming time. Or you can have a fine display of tulips: the short-stemmed Kaufmannianas (white and carmine) are in flower from March onwards. The trouble with bulbs is that you have to wait such a long time for the leaves to die down, for it is fatal to cut them. It is, therefore, an advantage to use the early-flowering ones if you must have them co-habiting with the roses.

You will certainly get early perfume with the jonquils, which grow about 30cm (1ft) tall and flower in April, and undoubtedly you will be enchanted by the delightful little *Narcissus minimus (asturiensis)*, one of the smallest – it grows only 7cm (3in) high – and flowering in February. A little taller is the well known yellow hoop petticoat narcissus, which normally blooms in March.

If you insist on having other flowering plants in the rose bed during summer, almost anything will satisfy your tastes. A lot depends on the

Above and top: 'Maigold' is worthily one of the most respected of our climbers. It bears rich orange-gold fragrant flowers early in the season and sometimes comes back with another flush of bloom. Very prickly, it grows to about 4m (13ft).

situation of the bed. If you have it close to a fence, so that it is more of a border, then you would be justified in having, say, some tall-growing hollyhocks or delphiniums at the back. And nobody would be likely to argue about sending roses and clematis climbing together up an old tree, or even a wall.

Different flowers can be used as a background for your roses. As if to compensate for the scarcity of a really attractive blue rose variety, there are some blue plants that make almost perfect companions. Lavender is an automatic choice; so is catmint, and some of the campanulas (notably *C. lactiflora*) are particularly good. Geraniums (pelargoniums, if you prefer) provide their own earthy tang and generally grow low enough not to get in the way – but be careful to avoid a colour clash with your roses. Pinks and carnations, with their unusual leaf shape and colour and individual perfume, can also make a useful contribution to the beauty of the scene. Silver foliage plants such as senecio (or cineraria) and *Stachys lanata* will likewise provide a pleasing colour combination.

Some excellent effects can be achieved using mainly herbaceous plants interspersed with roses, but in these cases the roses are merely providing the accompaniment, as it were, not being the chief performers.

The point is that the roses and their companions should complement each other. This will guarantee the harmony that hallmarks the garden of a true lover of plants and flowers.

Roses add beauty and elegance to the garden, whether on their own or in combination with other plants. Here climbing roses (opposite), honeysuckle and clematis curtain an old stone wall, and (above) floribundas and herbaceous perennials together make an attractive display.

# Acknowledgments

Photographs and illustrations were supplied or are reproduced by kind permission of the following:

A–Z Collection: 18 top, 24 top and bottom, 45, 57, 121 top, 144 bottom left

B. Alfieri: 76, 78 top

Heather Angel: 32, 114, 115 top, 130 top, 135 top

Ardea Photographics: 7, 22–3, 46–7

Andrzej Bielicki: 55

Pat Brindley: 4 centre, 18 bottom, 19, 20 top left and right, bottom, 21, 26 top, 30 top, 32–3, 41 top, 52 top and bottom, 54 top, 59, 61 top and bottom, 69, 78 bottom, 79, 82, 84 top, 85 bottom, 86 top and bottom, 87 top, 89 bottom, 96, 108 bottom left, 110, 137 bottom, 143, 145 bottom

Peter Coats: 58, 66

Bruce Coleman: 8, 141 (Jane Burton)

R. J. Corbin: 27, 62, 77 top, 87 bottom

John Cowley: 130 bottom

Ernest Crowson: 83, 88, 127 right

Dobies: 42–3

Valerie Finnis: 31, 73, 85 top, 147

Nancy-Mary Goodall: 1

Iris Hardwick Library: 135 bottom

Anthony Huxley: 37

G. E. Hyde: 64 top left, 77 bottom

IGDA: 124

Leslie Johns: 10, 26 bottom, 64 bottom

Sally Launder: 53

Elsa Megson: 121 bottom

Tania Midgley: 38, 139 top

Pictor International: 2–3, 28, 80, 104–5

Royal National Rose Society: 139 bottom right

Kenneth Scowen: endpapers, 6, 25, 35, 40, 92, 123, 127 left, 128, 140

Harry Smith Photographic Collection: 4 bottom, 5 top and bottom, 11, 12, 13, 15, 16–17, 29, 34 top, 36 bottom, 39, 41 bottom, 44, 49, 54 bottom, 60 left and right, 64 top right, 65, 67, 74, 75 top, 81 top and bottom, 89 top, 93, 94, 97, 100, 102, 106, 108 top and bottom right, 109, 112 bottom, 117, 118 top, 119 left, 120, 122 right, 129, 136, 137 top, 138 top and bottom, 139 bottom left, 142, 145 top, 146

P. Stiles: 50

W. J. Unwin Ltd: 36 top

R Verey: 68

Michael Warren: 4 top, 5 centre, 71, 90, 91, 95, 101, 107, 112 top, 113, 115 bottom, 116 top, 118 bottom, 121 centre, 122 left, 125, 126

D. Wildrige: 111

All possible care has been taken in tracing the ownership of copyright material used in this book and in making acknowledgment for its use. If any owner has not been acknowledged the publishers apologize and will be glad of the opportunity to rectify the error.

Pictorial diagrams on pages 8, 9, 48, 72, 100 and 134 by Tudor Art Agency Ltd
Information charts by Peter White

# Bibliography

Every gardening writer – and every gardening enthusiast – needs a bank of information on which he can draw freely and regularly. Over the years I must have consulted scores, if not hundreds, of specialist books and catalogues when seeking knowledge or checking facts. I gladly acknowledge my long-standing debt, and willingly share details of my store of information, by listing some of those publications I have consulted most often.

It is far from being the complete list, but those mentioned have become favourites because of either their vast range, or their compactness, or because it is easy for me to find my way about them. All are tried and trusted companions.

Doerflinger, Frederic, *The Bulb Book* (David & Charles, 1973)

Hellyer, A. G. L., *Collingridge Encyclopedia of Gardening* (Hamlyn, 1976)

Hillier, Harold G., *Manual of Trees and Shrubs* (David & Charles, 1974)

Hollis, Leonard, *Roses* (Hamlyn, 1974)

*Royal Horticultural Society Dictionary of Gardening* (Oxford University Press, 1956)

Sanders, T. W., *Encyclopedia of Gardening* (Hamlyn, 1957)

Thomas, Graham Stuart, *Plants for Ground Cover* (Dent, 1970)

CATALOGUES

Chatto, Beth, *Unusual Plants*, Elmstead Market, Colchester, Essex

*Cramphorn Planting Guide*, Cuton Mill, Chelmsford, Essex

*Jackman's Planter's Handbook*, Jackman's Nurseries, Woking, Surrey

Notcutts Nurseries, Woodbridge, Suffolk

Dobie, Samuel, and Son, Llangollen, Clwyd, Wales

Sunningdale Nurseries, Windlesham, Surrey

Suttons Seeds Ltd, Torquay, Devon

Thompson & Morgan, Ipswich, Suffolk

Unwin, W. J., Histon, Cambridge

# Index